A Cultural History
of the
United States

■

Through the Decades

The 1970s

Gail B. Stewart

Lucent Books, Inc., San Diego, California

19.95 Unique 8/99

Library of Congress Cataloging-in-Publication Data

Stewart, Gail, 1949–
    The 1970s / by Gail B. Stewart.
        p.   cm.—(A cultural history of the United States through
the decades)
    Includes bibliographical references and index.
    Summary: Discusses the political, economic, and cultural life of
the United States in the 1970s, including Vietnam, race relations,
feminism, the environment, fashion, music, television, and film.
    ISBN 1-56006-557-5 (alk. paper)
    1. United States—Civilization—1970– —Juvenile literature.
2. United States—History—1969– —Juvenile literature.
3. Nineteen seventies—Juvenile literature. [1. Nineteen seventies.
2. United States—History—1969– 3. United States—Social life
and customs—1971–   ] I. Title. II. Series.
E169.12.S837   1999
973.924—dc21   98-24585
                                                                     CIP
                                                                      AC

Copyright 1999 by Lucent Books, Inc.
P.O. Box 289011, San Diego, California 92198-9011

120508   Printed in the U.S.A.

Contents

Introduction: A Coming of Age. 5

Chapter One: A House Divided:

  Politics in the Seventies. 8

Chapter Two: "I Am Woman; Hear Me Roar" 24

Chapter Three: A Piece of the Pie. 36

Chapter Four: Energy and the Environment 49

Chapter Five: "No Rules" Rule:

  Fashion and Fads in the Seventies 63

Chapter Six: Music of the Seventies. 76

Chapter Seven: Television and Film in the Seventies 89

Epilogue: A Final Thought 107

Notes 109

Chronology 115

For Further Reading 117

Works Consulted. 119

Index 123

Picture Credits. 127

About the Author. 128

(From left to right) Feminists Bella Abzug, Gloria Steinem, and Betty Friedan march in support of the Equal Rights Amendment. Women's fight for equal treatment in the workplace began in earnest during the 1970s.

A Coming of Age

As decades go, the 1970s has been the cause of little reflection or study. The decade lacks the danger and flair of the '20s, the sacrifice and tragedy of the war years of the '40s, or the dismal hard times of the '30s.

The '70s are the years of disco, polyester leisure suits, CB radios, and pet rocks—a time that many feel was vapid and self-absorbed. One historian writes sarcastically:

The '70s image of hard times? John Travolta in *Saturday Night Fever* gazing through a store window at platform shoes he can't afford and yelling at his father, "Would you just watch the hair? You know, I work on my hair a long time, and you just hit it."[1]

The Problem with the Seventies

In contrast, the previous decade was exciting. During the 1960s, millions of Americans marched against the visible enemies of racism and discrimination. Those coming of age in the 1960s—especially in the early years of the decade—believed they were making a difference. Says one history teacher,

It was as if anything and everything was possible. We could join the Peace Corps to make a visible difference, or demonstrate with others, marching for civil rights. Those of us who were coming of age in the 60s all believed that we could do what no generation could ever have done; we were going to be the ones to set the world on its ear.[2]

Like the younger sibling of a particularly gifted and talented child, the '70s have been rigorously compared to the wildly exciting decade that came before it, and has been found wanting. The problem with the '70s, unfortunately, is that they weren't the '60s. But a closer look at the '70s will show that a great deal happened during these years.

John Travolta dances to a disco beat in Saturday Night Fever. *Disco music and dancing were popular in the 1970s.*

In *Very Seventies: A Cultural History of the 1970s from the Pages of Crawdaddy*, Peter Knobler and Greg Mitchell note that "The '70s couldn't begin until the 60s had been killed off."[3] In many ways, the '70s were the years that defined how we coped with the demise of things we valued. The murders of four college students by government troops all but ended student antiwar protests. The faith America had in its government stopped with the revelations of Watergate. Even the 1970 breakup of the Beatles signaled the end of an era.

The decade of the '70s was a time of beginnings—often in fits and starts, but beginnings nonetheless. They were the years when television grew up and the environment became an issue for the first time. It was a time of tremendous strides in the women's movement, and Native Americans became a recognizable political force. Indeed, as one historian points out, although many in the '70s were eager to pronounce the activism of the '60s dead, they were misguided: "If one looked just a bit below the surface, there was massive evidence that . . . people were on the move organizing . . . in small towns and obscure places that had never seen such things before."[4]

America was definitely a different place in the 1970s than it had been in the '60s. How we came of age after the '60s is a fascinating adventure in politics, social activism, and cultural history—polyester and all.

Chapter One

American troops arrive on the Mekong Delta during the Vietnam War. As the war dragged on during the early 1970s Americans grew more frustrated with the protracted conflict.

A House Divided: Politics in the Seventies

No single issue shaped the early 1970s as much as the war in Vietnam. Not only did the war dominate U.S. foreign policy, it virtually controlled the domestic climate, too. Whether or not Americans agreed with U.S. involvement in Vietnam, or supported politicians who agreed with U.S. involvement, the war shaped the way Americans defined themselves and one another.

By 1970 the war had been raging for thirteen years—longer than that, if one counted Vietnam's struggle against

France for its independence. In its early stages, U.S. involvement had been only advisory. President Harry Truman had sent a team of military consultants to aid the French. President Eisenhower had increased the aid, offering to send U.S. military officers to train the South Vietnamese army.

During the Kennedy administration American advisory presence in Vietnam increased to more than seventeen thousand. Kennedy had misgivings about the country's involvement in a foreign war, perhaps foreseeing a difficult situation worsening for the United States. Just days before his assassination in Dallas, Kennedy told an aide, "I want you to organize an in-depth study of every possible option we've got in Vietnam, including how to get out of there."[5]

Although early in his administration President Lyndon Johnson vowed that he would not increase involvement in Southeast Asia, the number of soldiers sent to Vietnam increased substantially. Like Kennedy—as well as Eisenhower and Truman—Johnson believed that it would be dangerous to allow the Communists a foothold in Southeast Asia. If the Communists were successful in taking over Vietnam, the reasoning went, other nations in that part of the world would fall like dominoes.

In 1965 the first American combat troops were sent to Vietnam, and although Johnson continued to assure the American people that this was a very short-lived activity, the war continued to escalate. U.S. forces totalled about 184,000 in 1965; by 1967 there were 427,000 American troops in Vietnam, and 6,600 had been killed in action.

"Not Months, but Weeks"

Yet as the war continued with no signs of stopping, President Johnson and his military advisors were optimistic in their assurances to the

American troops patrol the beaches of Vietnam in 1965. They were some of the first troops sent to Vietnam.

American people. "The Viet Cong [Communist guerrilla fighters] are going to collapse within weeks," said National Security Advisor Walt Rostow. "Not months, but weeks."[6]

By the election of 1968 it was clear that Johnson's optimism about the war was unfounded. The Viet Cong had mounted a powerful offensive and more U.S. troops were shipped overseas. More and more Americans were angry about their nation's involvement in a war taking place in a little country thousands of miles away. College campuses buzzed with antiwar demonstrations; students protested the killing in Vietnam by chanting: "Hey, hey, LBJ! How many kids did you kill today?"

Even those who had supported the war were uneasy, for it seemed that millions of dollars and thousands of lives were being spent, with no clear victory in sight. By the end of 1968 the United States had dropped more bombs on Vietnam than it had during all of World War II. Seeing voter support waning, President Johnson had decided against running for a second term in 1968. In January 1969, Re-

Richard Nixon (right) is sworn in as president by Chief Justice Earl Warren (left). Nixon's wife, Pat, is in the center. Although Nixon promised to end the war in Vietnam immediately, he initially committed more troops to the effort.

publican Richard Nixon was sworn in as president.

Bombing Cambodia

During the campaign, Nixon had stressed the need for peace in Vietnam. He said that he was sure that he could do what President Johnson had not been able to do—end the war quickly. "I pledge to you," he said to the voters, "new leadership will end the war and win the peace in the Pacific."[7]

Just how he intended to achieve peace must be kept secret, he stressed, for he did not want to compromise his bargaining position by revealing strategy before the election. All he needed, he promised, was six months' time to end the war.

But early in 1970 it became clear that Nixon could not keep his promise. Not only did he not decrease U.S. military activity in Vietnam, he authorized an expansion of the war into neutral Cambodia, where it was believed that the Viet Cong had built military bases. In a televised speech to the American people from the Oval Office at 9:00 P.M. on April 30, Nixon explained why he felt that the invasion was necessary.

He said that it was critically important for the United States to show

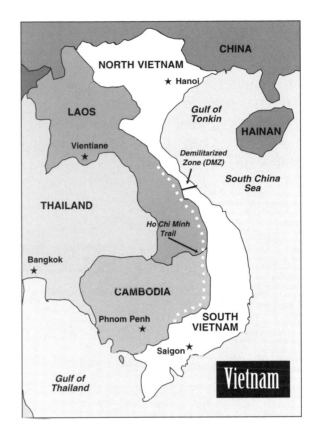

that it would not be weakened or humiliated by the Communists of North Vietnam. "If, when the chips are down," he warned, "the world's most powerful nation, the United States of America, acts like a pitiful, helpless giant, the forces of totalitarianism and anarchy will threaten free nations . . . throughout the world."[8]

Angry Reactions

Many reacted with anger, especially surprised senators who had known nothing about the invasion. Said Senator Ted Kennedy, "This is madness." Another senator called Nixon's warlike actions "a declaration of war against the Senate."[9] And Majority Leader Mike Mansfield declared, "It is a difficult situation to reconcile one's mind to. . . . The outlook seems to be getting grimmer by the day."[10]

Opposition to the war had been growing because of increased television coverage, too. Network news crews, along with cameras, were bringing the war in vivid, horrifying detail into American living rooms, something that had never happened before. "People were forced to see the bodies, the blood," comments one observer. "Vietnam wasn't just a politician's war—real people were dying, and unless you lived in a cave, your television made you aware of it every evening at six o'clock."[11]

The Pentagon Papers

In this excerpt from American Decades: 1970–1979, *editor Victor Bondi explains the relevance of the Pentagon Papers as they pertained to the scandal associated with Nixon's White House.*

"No one person was more influenced by the debates over the morality of the war in Vietnam than former Defense Department expert Daniel Ellsberg. A Vietnam hawk and former Marine who had been a member of Kissinger's advisory staff, Ellsberg was convinced by 1970 that the war was immoral and unconscionable. In order to expose what he believed were lies about the war, in June 1971 Ellsberg passed copies of a secret 1968 Defense Department history of Vietnam to the *New York Times.* The history, known as the Pentagon Papers, caused an uproar.

Many were scandalized by the extent to which the government had deceived the public about the reality of the war in Vietnam. Others argued that Ellsberg had betrayed the government. Even though the Pentagon Papers said nothing about the Nixon administration, the president and his staff, concerned about breaches in governmental security and concerned that the papers would undermine public confidence in their Vietnam policy, won a court injunction to prevent the *New York Times* from publishing them. On June 30, 1971, however, the Supreme Court overturned the injunction and upheld the right of the newspaper to publish the documents.

President Nixon, infuriated by the Supreme Court decision . . . responded by attacking Ellsberg. . . . The White House formed what it termed a "nonlegal team" to investigate Ellsberg and amass evidence to discredit him. The team, called the "plumbers unit" because it plugged governmental leaks, used illegal wiretaps to amass information on Ellsberg. . . . The White House . . . was so pleased with the activities of the plumbers unit that it became a permanent part of the president's staff. It was this group that would conduct the Watergate break-in in 1972."

The outrage was even stronger, however, on college campuses—a fact that surprised neither Nixon nor Vice President Agnew. Nixon had never been popular with student demonstrators, whom he labeled "bums." Vice President Spiro Agnew was even more vocal in his condemnation of students. He said they were troublemakers, the same as Nazis or Ku Klux Klan members. "Just imagine they are wearing brown shirts or white sheets," he advised law enforcement officials, "and act accordingly."[12]

The expansion of the war increased student activism enormously. In addition to being outraged over the war's expansion, college students were furious at the indiscriminate nature of the destruction. The bombing and spraying of poisonous chemicals such as Agent Orange not only killed North Vietnamese soldiers; innocent civilians were killed as well. (The randomness of the killing in Vietnam was already a sore spot, since the 1968 massacre of two hundred civilians at the little South Vietnamese village of My Lai came to light. Led by Lt. William Calley, whose subsequent trial resulted in his murder conviction, the My Lai incident was a shameful reminder to all Americans of the atrocities that occurred in war.)

Students were not the only ones to react angrily to the Cambodia invasion. On May 4, the presidents of thirty-seven colleges and universities—among them Notre Dame, Columbia, Dartmouth, New York University, and Princeton—sent a letter of protest to President Nixon. They implored him to end the war quickly, warning that he needed to consider "the incalculable dangers of an unprecedented alienation of America's youth."[13]

Tragedy at Kent State

On May 1, students at a small Ohio university called Kent State staged a demonstration against the invasion of Cambodia. Some students smashed windows in downtown Kent, protesting what they felt was the establishment's support of the war. A Reserve Officers' Training Corp (ROTC) building on campus was burned, too.

The mayor of Kent urged Governor James Rhodes to send in national guardsmen to help restore order. The next day students and faculty alike were stunned to see the Ohio National Guard, in full battle gear, advancing onto their campus. With gas masks, loaded rifles and bayonets, they came mounted on jeeps and army trucks, while the students yelled insults at them.

Governor Rhodes also came to Kent State. He called a news conference and verbally attacked the students as troublemakers and dissidents. "We're going to use every weapon of the law-enforcement agencies of Ohio," he warned, "to drive them out of Kent."[14]

Just after noon on May 4, as masses of students gathered to protest, shots rang out. At least ten of the guardsmen had fired into a crowd of students in a parking area more than one hundred yards away. Fifteen students were hit; four were killed. Screaming in terror, the students fled from the soldiers.

One eighteen-year-old witness tells what she saw:

> I saw the men firing, and I saw the kids fall, and I looked out at the crowd and there were people . . . with blood all over them down the hill, and I just couldn't believe it. I've never seen people so mad and so horrified. . . . There's no way to describe the pain that I saw in people's faces.[15]

A Nation Horrified

The event at Kent State horrified the nation. Many spoke out against those antiwar demonstrators who had smashed windows and burned the ROTC building on campus. They agreed with the earlier statements of the president and vice president, who

called such demonstrators "troublemakers" and "bums."

Many others were furious that the National Guard treated college students like criminals and terrorists. They noted that of the thirteen students shot, eleven had been hit in the side or back, proving that they had been running away, not advancing toward the guardsmen, as had been earlier claimed by guard spokesmen. In addition, it was discovered that of the four who had been killed, none had even been involved with the protest.

The response of the administration did nothing to calm the American

National Guardsmen at Kent State University are shown shortly before they begin firing into the crowd of demonstrators, leaving four students dead and several others injured.

people. In a press conference Nixon had no words of sympathy for the families of the dead and wounded students. "This should remind us all once again," the president said, "that when dissent turns to violence, it invites tragedy."[16]

Violence in New York

Within a few days of the tragedy, students nationwide launched demonstrations against what they saw as government brutality and a limiting of their right to protest. In what was the first-ever student strike in U.S. history, more than 450 colleges and universities shut down.

More violence erupted in New York City on May 7, when Mayor John Lindsay lowered the flag over City Hall to half-mast to pay tribute to the deaths at Kent State. More than a thousand hard-hat construction workers—many of them veterans and all supporters of the Vietnam war—invaded City Hall to demand that the flag be raised.

Students who had gathered there for a rally were attacked, and seventy

The "Me" Decade?

In his book Chronicle of America, *editor Clifton Daniel includes an article that attempts to label the 1970s as the "Me" decade, because of people's apparent lack of concern about anything but their own needs. This is an excerpt from that article.*

"Writing in *New York* magazine, satirist Tom Wolfe has called this the 'Me Decade.' Chronologically, 1976 is smack in the middle of 'me-ness,' and there are some statistics to bear Wolfe out. One report reveals three out of five marriages end in divorce, and one out of five children lives in a one-parent home.

Is it a coincidence that teenage SAT scores are so low? What were parents doing while their children's average scores dropped to 472 in math and 453 in English (from 501 and 480 in 1968)? Perhaps they were joining the Me generation, filling up on bran to live longer (bran cereal sales climbed 20 percent this year), or worrying more about the numbers on their paychecks than those on their kids' tests.

No longer, it seems, are people willing to risk life and limb to march for peace, harmony, and civil rights. Unless, of course, the price is right."

were beaten with clubs and fists while police turned their backs. Construction workers carried signs reading: "Get the Hippies" and "Get Out of America." One construction worker expressed the anger he felt toward the students who

A "Flop" of the Seventies

One of the least successful innovations of the 1970s was created by the U.S. government—the Susan B. Anthony dollar. In 1978 Congress authorized the U.S. Mint to begin issuing coins with the likeness of Anthony, a pioneer in women's rights. The coin marked the first time a woman (other than a mythical one, such as the Statue of Liberty) appeared on a U.S. coin.

Both sides of the dollar coin were designed by the then chief engraver of the U.S. Mint, Frank Gasparro. His initials appear below the portrait of Susan B. Anthony. The issuance of the Susan B. Anthony dollar was something of a novelty, as is the introduction of any new money into circulation. However, it did not take long for people to dislike it.

For one thing, it was light. It was made of copper and nickel on the outer layer, with an inner core of copper, so it did not "feel" as though it were worth a dollar. Most annoying, however, was the coin's small size; it often caused confusion with a quarter. For these reasons, the Susan B. Anthony dollar slid quietly out of use, and by 1981, it was no longer minted.

The Susan B. Anthony dollar was a flop from the start. The new coins could be easily mistaken for quarters.

were protesting the war: "We put our sweat and blood into building this city. Now these punks want to bring it all down with bombs and riots. They ain't American. Send 'em to Russia. This is our city and our country. We built it!"[17]

Soon after the violence in New York, President Nixon invited Peter Brennan, the head of the construction workers' union, to a reception at the White House. Brennan brought an honorary hard hat for the president, and Nixon reciprocated by pinning an American flag on Brennan's lapel. Historian Jules Archer writes, "The president thus made it clear that he favored letting mob violence suppress antiwar demonstrations."[18]

As the American people watched their evening news reports during the spring of 1970, it seemed as though there was no good news at all. The war was escalating, there were riots and fighting on American soil, and the nation seemed more divided than in any time in recent memory. One reporter for the *New York Times* wrote, "America was in anguish last week— her population divided, her campuses closed, her capital shaken, her government confused, her president perplexed."[19]

Vietnamization and Negotiation

Soon after taking office, Nixon had proposed a program he called "Vietnamization" as a way of ending the war. His idea was to gradually remove U.S. troops from Vietnam while training South Vietnamese troops to take over. Vietnamization was progressing slowly, however, and seemed to take a backseat at times to stepped-up attacks by the United States on Communist forces in Vietnam.

Nixon also hoped to hear good news from his national security advisor, Henry Kissinger, who had been trying to negotiate a settlement with the North Vietnamese. Those negotiations, too, seemed to be going nowhere.

By 1972 Nixon was well aware of the American people's impatience. Those against the war, of course,

wanted U.S. troops to pull out immediately. However, even those who supported the war were frustrated. They believed that the United States somehow had its hands tied—that Nixon was not using enough military force. If we were going to fight, they said, then let's win the war and get out.

Two Historic Journeys

Hoping to turn public attention from Vietnam, Nixon made two historic journeys in 1972. The first was to China, remarkable because it was the first time an American president had ever visited there. When the Communists came to power in 1949, the United States severed diplomatic relations with China. But in 1972, Nixon met with Chinese leaders and visited farms and communes. Although there was no earth-shattering improvement in U.S.-China relations, the door was left open for further meetings.

Nixon's second trip was to the Soviet Union to meet with Chairman Leonid Brezhnev. In the first-ever summit in Moscow between an American and Soviet president, Nixon was allowed to address the Soviet people on television. In a speech that many historians feel was one of his best, he attacked the fear, which he said undermined relations between the Soviet Union and America:

Richard Nixon and wife Pat (center) on their historic trip to China. Nixon was most successful in developing diplomatic relations with China and the Soviet Union.

Through all the pages of history, through all the centuries, the world's peoples have struggled to be free from fear, whether fear of the elements or hunger, or fear of their own rulers, or fear of their neighbors in other countries. And yet time and again, people have vanquished the source of one fear only to fall prey to another. Let our goal now be a world without fear.[20]

Nixon's accomplishments in diplomatic relations during both the China and Soviet Union trips continue to be viewed as his biggest contribution to the presidency.

The positive response he received from the China trip and the Moscow summit, together with his assurances of ongoing negotiations with North Vietnam, helped Nixon during the election of 1972.

His opponent in that election was forty-nine-year-old George McGovern, a soft-spoken Democratic senator from South Dakota. McGovern was a fierce critic of U.S. involvement in Vietnam, and had harshly criticized Nixon's expansion of the war into Cambodia.

A Suspicious Break-In

Although the presidential campaign of 1972 has been mostly forgotten because of McGovern's poor showing in November, it remains noteworthy because of a burglary that occurred during the summer before the election. On June 17, 1972, five men were arrested and charged with burglary at the Democratic National Committee headquarters at the Watergate, a downtown Washington hotel, apartment, and office complex. One of the men, James McCord, was a former FBI agent. The burglars were in the Democratic headquarters fixing electronic eavesdropping equipment that they had planted during a previous break-in. Curiously, papers found on the men indicated that they worked for the Committee to Re-Elect the President—an agency which would be known sarcastically as CREEP.

The break-in at the Watergate did not grab headlines that summer. Although the connection between the burglary and CREEP had been established, the White House scoffed at the idea that the Nixon administration had had anything to do with it. As Nixon's press secretary Ron

---

Death Row for a Killer

One of the most talked-about trials of the '70s was that of Charles Manson and three members of his "family." Manson, a thirty-five-year-old ex-con who had been in and out of prison since he was thirteen, was the charismatic leader of a hippie cult which dwelled twenty miles outside of Los Angeles. The cult members—young women who worshipped Manson—were heavy users of LSD and other drugs.

On August 9, 1969, Manson and three of the young women savagely murdered actress Sharon Tate, the wife of director Roman Polanski, and three guests at her home. A passerby was also killed. Tate was eight months pregnant. There appeared to be no motive for the killings; nothing was stolen, and Manson and his cult members did not know the people they killed. The word "pig" was scrawled in blood on the door.

The trial, which lasted 121 days, ended on January 25, 1971, as Manson and the three codefendants were found guilty. Those who followed the trial commented on the uncanny, eerily bright eyes of Manson and the women. They were sentenced to death, although when the Supreme Court suspended the death penalty in 1972 their sentences were changed to life in prison. Interestingly, Manson has remained one of the most popular prisoners on death row, receiving thousands of letters from adoring young women each year.

Ziegler scornfully told reporters during a news conference, "I'm not going to comment on a third-rate burglary attempt."[21]

Investigations and Denials

No matter what Ziegler said, however, George McGovern and his campaign staff were furious, insisting that the White House had to have been involved. But the public did not seem interested. Why would President Nixon and the Republicans bother bugging the Democratic headquarters when McGovern posed no threat? Besides, writes one historian, the public perceived that "dirty tricks in an election year was almost a national tradition."[22]

There were some, however, who wouldn't let the incident disappear, even after McGovern was defeated in the election. Two reporters for the *Washington Post,* Carl Bernstein and Bob Woodward, painstakingly followed the paper trail from McCord and the other burglars, and claimed that it led to members of the president's own staff. The pressure Bernstein and Woodward applied in their investigation forced Nixon to call his own investigation into the matter.

However, Nixon announced on April 30, 1973, that his legal counsel, John Dean, had determined that there

was no wrongdoing whatsoever on the part of the White House. "I can say categorically," he stated in a televised address to the nation, "that [Dean's] investigation indicates that no one in the White House staff, no one in this administration presently employed, was involved in this bizarre incident."[23]

The Presidency Unravels

But while Nixon was busy assuring Americans that he and his staff were not involved in the break-in and the wiretapping of the office at the Watergate, some people close to the president were arranging payoffs to those arrested, in exchange for their silence.

As more and more evidence was discovered, it became clear that the Nixon administration was definitely involved in wrongdoing. What had seemed unthinkable back in June of 1972—presidential knowledge of a plan of wiretapping, eavesdropping, and burglary—was a reality. In a national speech, Nixon insisted, "People have got to know whether or not their president is a crook. Well, I am not a crook."[24] Those words would haunt Nixon.

In May 1973 the Senate Select Committee on Presidential Campaign Activities, chaired by North Carolina senator Sam Ervin, began holding hearings on the Watergate affair. The star witness was former presidential counsel John Dean, who admitted his active role in the cover-up, and charged that President Nixon had known about all of it. The break-in at the Watergate, it was revealed, was only one of the many "dirty tricks" carried out by Nixon's staff on his behalf.

Over the next months, Nixon's presidency continued to unravel. In July 1973 the White House chief of staff revealed that the president regularly taped conversations in the Oval Office. For more than a year Nixon tried to keep the tapes secret, but eventually a Supreme Court decision forced him to turn over the tapes to prosecutors.

Stepping Down

The tapes showed a side of President Nixon that shocked even his most ardent supporters. Said the *New York Times*, the tapes

> showed a president who was profane, indecisive . . . concerned more with saving his own skin than getting at the truth, and deeply involved in discussions about employing perjury and hush money to insulate himself from scandal.[25]

In July 1974 the House Judiciary Committee recommended impeachment, accusing Nixon both of

obstructing justice in the scandal and of abusing presidential powers. Because the tapes indicated his knowledge of the cover-up from almost the beginning, Nixon knew he had no remaining support in his party.

In a speech to the American people on August 8, 1974, Nixon explained that he would resign the next day. Vice President Gerald Ford succeeded him. (Ford had been appointed by Nixon in October 1973 when Spiro Agnew had been forced to resign in shame for taking bribes.)

Gerald Ford and wife Betty (left) and Richard and Pat Nixon leave the White House after Nixon's resignation.

Jimmy Carter

Ford finished out Nixon's second term, but could not command the confidence of the American people. Ford angered many people, too, when he granted a full pardon to Nixon a month following his resignation. It surprised no one, therefore, when Ford was defeated in the election of 1976.

The thirty-ninth president of the United States was former Georgia governor Jimmy Carter. Carter appealed to many voters because he had *not* served in Washington, D.C. The American people had had enough of the corruption that surrounded the Nixon administration, and Carter became something of a symbol of hope that government could be run honestly.

Carter gained popularity for his role in a historic Middle East peace treaty. He met with Prime Minister Menachim Begin of Israel and President Anwar Sadat of Egypt at Camp David, the presidential retreat in Maryland, beginning on September 6, 1978. After twelve days the three emerged from the negotiations to an-nounce that they had agreed to a "framework for peace" between Egypt and Israel.

A Bicentennial Feeling

America's two-hundredth birthday was celebrated on July 4, 1976 (the anniversary of the signing of the Declaration of Independence, rather than the patriots' victory over the British). Although it was a fairly gloomy time in national and world affairs, writes Peter Carroll in It Seemed Like Nothing Happened: The Tragedy and Promise of America in the 1970s, *there was a sense of patriotic pride that added to the occasion.*

"On July 4, 1976, President Ford presented a series of patriotic speeches. 'Liberty is a living flame to be fed, not dead ashes to be revered,' he remarked at Independence Hall, 'even in a Bicentennial Year.' But most people paid more attention to a dramatic flotilla of sailing vessels in New York harbor, watched gigantic fireworks displays, heard the jazzy arrangements of Arthur Fiedler and the Boston Pops. 'The feeling of the day sort of crept up on many of us, took us by surprise,' noticed [columnist] Elizabeth Drew. 'For those of us who had been in despair about this Bicentennial, . . . who feared the worst, the surprise was a very pleasant one. But,' she emphasized, 'it was a people's day. . . . No doubt the good feeling one observed today, even the patriotic feeling, comes out of confidence in our country, as distinguished from confidence in our government.'"

Jimmy Carter was elected president in 1976. His presidency was marked by economic and foreign policy troubles.

But the Camp David accords, as the framework was known, was one of the few positive aspects of Carter's presidency. A critical gas shortage occurred soon after he took office, and double-digit inflation began in 1978.

The Iran Hostage Crisis

But the most damaging event to Carter's presidency was his failure to resolve the hostage crisis in Iran. On November 4, 1979, thousands of anti-U.S. revolutionaries stormed the American Embassy in Tehran, Iran. Fifty-three Americans were imprisoned, and would not be released, said the revolutionaries, until the United States turned over the shah of Iran to them so he could be put on trial for crimes against the Iranian people. The shah, whose U.S.-supported government had been overthrown six months before, was in the United States undergoing medical treatment.

The takeover of the embassy, writes one historian, "confronted Carter with a challenge to U.S. prestige and his administration's resourcefulness in dealing with a radical regime's defiance of American rights."[26] Unfortunately, the challenge was too much.

Carter refused to meet the demands of the revolutionaries, and promptly seized eight billion dollars in Iranian deposits in U.S. banks. He also ordered navy warships to be on alert near Iran. However, neither strategy worked, and the crisis dragged on—not to be ended until Carter's presidency was through. The episode, writes one observer, "suggested a paralysis of will and an embarrassing failure of the country's power."[27] It was a disturbing political note on which to end the decade of the 1970s.

Chapter Two

Women celebrate the fifty-first anniversary of women's suffrage in 1971. These women chant out slogans while demanding "51 percent of everything"—the rights they believe should reflect their majority in the population.

"I Am Woman; Hear Me Roar"

The 1960s was characterized by a great deal of social rebellion and upheaval. In the early part of the decade, much of it was centered around black Americans' demands for civil rights; in the latter part, it was the cry for an end to the war in Vietnam.

It was a time, too, when women were realizing that they held a second-class place in society. For instance, although women made up about one-third of the American workforce, they were usually employed in low-income, dead-end jobs. Society was still teaching little girls that there was no higher, more fulfilling goal than to marry and have children. And while those goals were just right for some girls, for others they were frustratingly limited.

"Move on, Little Girl"

The 1967 publication of *The Feminine Mystique*, by Betty Friedan, brought the frustration women were feeling into the open. One historian writes:

> At one stroke, [Friedan] exploded the simplistic myth of women as happy little homemakers. Arguments raged over [her] insistence that women were intensely dissatisfied with . . . subordinating their own needs . . . to the needs of husbands, and with their lack of equal opportunity in the workplace.[28]

The growing cry for equal rights for women did not receive much support from either the civil rights or antiwar groups. Hoping—and perhaps being confident—that their struggle for equal rights would be respected by black leaders or the antiwar groups, women found themselves ignored or taken for granted when they tried to participate. According to one historian, women in social action organizations "most frequently licked envelopes and washed dishes while the men planned strategy and gave speeches."[29]

Those women who objected to such roles were often ridiculed. In 1964, for example, when women in a campus activist organization called the Student Nonviolent Coordinating Committee (SNCC) tried to deliver a paper on the position of women in that organization, one of the leaders quipped, "The only position for women in SNCC is prone."[30]

At another activist assembly in Chicago in 1967, a feminist speaker named Shulamith Firestone tried to take the podium to talk about women's demands. Instead, the chairman of the convention was patronizing to her. "[He] patted her on the head. 'Move on, little girl,' he said. 'We have more important issues to talk about here than women's liberation.'"[31]

Strength in Being Separate

By the end of the 1960s, therefore, women's organizations were realizing that they would be better off separating themselves from other groups. Women's liberation groups grew in numbers and in strength, as women in all segments of the population discovered that they could have a voice. They also learned that they had common goals, such as equality in jobs, education, child care, and abortion rights.

On August 26, 1970, one of the largest-ever events in the women's movement took place. Named by its organizers the "Women's Strike for Equality," the event marked the fiftieth anniversary of the day women

While president of the National Organization for Women (NOW), Betty Friedan organized a massive women's strike in New York City in 1970.

across America at the same time.

In organizing the march, explains one historian, "Betty asked secretaries to put covers on their typewriters, telephone operators to unplug their switchboards, waitresses to stop serving meals, cleaning women to put up their mops, and wives to stop cooking and making love that night."[32]

Many of the marchers carried placards reading "I AM NOT A BARBIE DOLL," "REPENT, MALE CHAUVINISTS—YOUR WORLD IS COMING TO AN END," and "DON'T CALL ME DOLL, CHICK, GIRL, OR BROAD." It was, Friedan later remarked, a wonderful way to

> hit home our two goals. The personhood of women. Equality of opportunity. And in 24 hours we became a political movement—with a message, with troops to march, with clout to force politicians to listen, and eventually, to hear. We dove into the mainstream—and we've never left.[33]

won the right to vote in the United States. Betty Friedan, the event's organizer, planned the march of more than thirty-five thousand down Fifth Avenue in New York City, just as suffragettes had done back in 1920. In addition, other parades were held

Mixed Messages

Betty Friedan and other leaders were rightly concerned about their goal of "the personhood of women"—the necessity for women to be respected as people. For too long throughout history women had been viewed as property, or seen as objects, by society in general, and men in particular. Feminist leaders knew that this "de-objectifying" of women was an important goal.

Most importantly, the 1970 availability of Dr. John Rock's oral contraceptive—known as "the Pill"—made sex without fear of pregnancy possible. Young women could be in control of their bodies as never before; they could plan their education, career, and children as they wished.

The Pill also made sexual experimentation more prevalent—young men and women were having sexual relationships without marriage, and in record numbers. The idea of a young woman keeping her virginity until she married was not as important as it once was.

But rather than make women more independent and self-confident, the sexual revolution of the '60s had a surprising backlash. Remembers one feminist,

> Society seemed to equate "liberated" with "promiscuous." Instead of being viewed as people who wanted to take control of their lives—including their reproductive lives—we were seen as a group of potential willing sex partners for men. Because we had the Pill, we were *expected* to sleep with them. In a lot of ways, it was worse than before![34]

Historian Peter Carroll agrees:

> Most women [still] regarded sex not as an isolated act, but as an integral part of a loving relationship. The eagerness of men to engage in detached sexuality thus created enormous pressure for liberated women either to conform to male sexual standards or to appear prudish and unsexual.[35]

"Should a Gentleman Offer a Tiparillo to a Lady?"

The media of the 1970s—especially corporate advertising—contributed greatly to the mixed messages about women's liberation. For advertisers, liberated women seemed to be a whole new market. "The strong woman—engaged in the difficult task of adopting 'masculine' jobs and sexual behavior—was a new kind of consumer," writes one historian, "one who might feel especially insecure about losing her femininity."[36]

For these women, there were a whole range of new products, includ-

The Battle of the Sexes

One of the most televised events in 1973 was a tennis match. Dubbed "The Match of the Century," it featured a fifty-five-year-old former Wimbledon champion named Bobby Riggs against the hottest of women tennis players, Billie Jean King.

It began as a boast—a highly publicized one—from Riggs that he could beat *any* woman, simply because men were superior to women. How seriously he meant the challenge no one really knew, for Riggs was well known as a hustler and publicity seeker. He had beat a powerful Australian player, Margaret Court, earlier in the year, and he gloated that he could do it again.

King was the strongest opponent Riggs could possibly have faced. In 1973 she had just completed two very successful seasons, and had been named *Sports Illustrated*'s first-ever Sportswoman of the Year. She was also a feminist; she had fought the inequities between men's and women's tennis events. (In 1970 first prize for men's singles at the Italian Open, for example, was $7,500, while the women's winner would receive $600!)

She accepted Riggs's challenge in July, and set to work training for the match.

It was a made-for-media event. Millions of Americans watched on television, and the atmosphere at the Houston As-

Billie Jean King and Bobby Riggs face off in their historic tennis match in 1973. King beat Riggs in all three sets.

trodome was more like a Super Bowl than a tennis match. The Las Vegas odds were 5 to 2, in favor of Riggs. Taunting and teasing, Riggs hoped to put King off her game. But it was not to be. She won in three straight sets, 6-4, 6-3, 6-3.

ing perfumes "for the woman on the go," cosmetics, and hair coloring. "The message in the advertising was fairly obvious," says one observer. "If you wanted to compete with the big boys, you were in danger of looking like a man. If you wanted to look like a woman, you'd better buy this stuff!" [37]

For instance, one ad for a feminine deodorant spray warned, "Having a female body doesn't make you feminine." As one cynical writer quipped, "One would think that if having a woman's body didn't make you feminine spraying stuff on your crotch wouldn't do much good, either."[38]

Many feminists objected to such advertising, especially that which trivialized the women's movement. One controversial advertisement for a small filtered cigar called a Tiparillo actually claimed credit for women's liberation:

It began 10 years ago when we asked, "Should a gentleman offer a Tiparillo to a lady?" A lot's happened since then. Today, a gentleman not only offers a Tiparillo to a lady, but the lady is taking up the offer. Yes, times have changed. . . . Curvaceous young women are jockeys. Co-ed dorms are part of the education. [At the bottom of the page] Tiparillo: Maybe we started something.[39]

Roe v. Wade

The courts backed many of the goals of the women's movement in the 1970s. Feminists won the right for women not to be excluded from sitting on juries. In

People gather for a women's liberation demonstration at City Hall in Washington, D.C., in 1970. A major focus of the women's rights movement was the legalization of abortion in all fifty states.

addition, women were granted the same legal status as men when it came to administering estates and handling property. But the most controversial ruling came in 1973 in a Supreme Court case known as *Roe v. Wade*, which concerned the right of women to have abortions. Until then, the only justification for an abortion in any state was the need to save the mother's life.

Feminists had been calling for an end to laws forbidding abortion. They argued that women's bodies were theirs alone, and that no one else had the right to tell them they must bear a child against their will. Illegal abortions, or women who tried to perform the abortions themselves with coat hangers, knitting needles, or harmful chemicals, resulted in many deaths and serious injuries.

The case began in 1970, when a single, young, pregnant waitress in Texas (calling herself Jane Roe, a pseudonym), was denied an abortion under the laws of that state. She sued the Dallas County district attorney, Henry Wade, claiming that the Texas law violated her right to privacy, which she was guaranteed under the Bill of Rights and the Fourteenth Amendment to the Constitution.

In a 7-2 decision, the Supreme Court agreed with Jane Roe, determining that every woman is entitled to an abortion within the first three months of her pregnancy. State laws that prohibited abortions during the first three months were found unconstitutional. More than any other case, *Roe v. Wade* aroused strong passions on both sides.

Inequity in the Workplace

The gathering strength of the women's movement resulted in legislative gains, too. In 1970 employment and educational opportunities for women were far less than those of men. Most newspapers had classified ads separated into "Help, Men" and "Help, Women." It was not unusual for women to be turned down for jobs simply because of their sex.

At the beginning of the decade, nearly 90 percent of working women were employed in clerical, sales, service, factory, or plant jobs. Women who worked made approximately fifty-nine cents for every dollar earned by men. And in 1972 women workers had a median income of $6,256 less than men.

Women's leaders lobbied hard for legislation that would increase the opportunities for women. But there were obstacles—the notion that women were less capable than men prevailed, even in high places. For instance, a government spokesperson in the space industry commented, "Talk of

A Wide Range of Feminist Thought

In the early 1970s there was a great difference of opinion among feminists concerning the best method to end sex discrimination and to gain equal rights in society. Many feminists believed that society was completely corrupt because it was dominated by men, and therefore women's liberation could never occur until the power roles were reversed. Others were less radical, and believed equality could be attained by "working within the system." The following is an excerpt of a radical feminist position paper of 1970 that urged the overthrow of social mores considered basic by many. It is included in Judith Papachristou's Women Together: A History in Documents of the Women's Movement in the United States.

Women march for equal rights during the 1970s. Although all feminists wanted reform, many disagreed about how to achieve their goals.

"We seek the self-development of every individual woman. To accomplish this we must eliminate the institutions built on the myth of maternal instinct which prevent her self-development, i.e., those institutions which enforce the female role.

We must destroy love (an institution by definition), which is generally recognized as approval and acceptance. Love promotes vulnerability, dependence, possessiveness, susceptibility to pain, and prevents the full development of woman's human potential by directing all her energies outward in the interests of others. The family depends for its maintenance on the identification by the woman of her own desires and needs with the desires and needs of the others. Motherhood provides blind approval as a bribe in return for which the mother expects to live vicariously through the child.

Between husband and wife, love is a delusion in the female that she is both a giver and a receiver, i.e., she sacrifices to get approval from the male. Love is a self-defense developed by the female to prevent her from seeing her powerless situation: it arises from fear when contact with reality provides no alternative to powerlessness. It is protection from the violence of the violations by other men.

Heterosexual love is a delusion in yet another sense; it is a means of escape from the role system by way of approval from and of identification with the man, who has defined himself as humanity (beyond role)—she desires to be him. The identification of each woman's interests with those of a man prevents her from uniting with other women and seeing herself as a member of the class of women."

an American spacewoman makes me sick to my stomach."[40] The president, too, was less than supportive in his views on equality in employment. Early in 1972 Richard Nixon joked, "Let me make one thing perfectly clear. I wouldn't want to wake up next to a lady pipe fitter."[41]

Strides in Equal Opportunity

But even though such attitudes often prevailed during the 1970s, several important goals were attained in the area of equal opportunity and employment. The most notable was in amending a law that had been passed years earlier, called the Civil Rights Act of 1964. Signed into law by then-president Lyndon Johnson, the bill had made it illegal for employers to discriminate against individuals based on their race, sex, religion, or national origin.

The problem with the law was in the way it was enforced. The Equal Employment Opportunity Commission was far more interested in enforcing the "race, religion, or national origin" aspect of the law. Sexual discrimination, therefore, was left unchecked.

In 1972, after several years of pressure by feminist groups such as the National Organization for Women (NOW), the guidelines for enforcing the law were amended. The new guidelines stated that women could not be denied jobs on the presumption that they were less suited to a certain type of job than men, or because employers or coworkers preferred men. In addition, it was illegal for advertisements to specify "male" or "female."

There were other big changes in the kinds of opportunities available to women. Title IX of the 1972 Educational Amendments Act prohibited any college or university that received federal aid from discriminating against women. One of the key aspects of Title IX was its requirement that college athletic programs had to fund men's and women's programs equally. This resulted in scholarship opportunities for talented women athletes who could never before have attended college.

Basketball star Nancy Lieberman of Old Dominion University, explained in 1979 what Title IX had done for her and her teammates:

Without Title IX our basketball team would be ten steps behind where we are today. [Her team was the intercollegiate champion that year.] I couldn't have come to Old Dominion without a full scholarship, which is now equivalent to what the men get, and if we didn't have the money from Title IX to

"Aren't We Good Enough to Be Respected?"

After Title IX of the Education Amendments Act was passed, women's athletics on the college level were brought up to the level of men's athletics. As a result, high schools began expanding their programs, for they knew that their talented athletes could win scholarships to college. The following letter, reprinted in The Decade of Women: A *Ms.* History of the Seventies in Words and Pictures, *was written by a disappointed high school athlete in the early 1970s, before the enactment of the law.*

"I am in the ninth grade and on the girls' varsity basketball team at our school. I'm captain of the team and lead it in scoring, steals, and assists. I love basketball.

During our whole season this year we had only five games: we had to furnish rides to the games ourselves; we had to play in our gymsuits because we had no uniforms in which to play; we were able to use the gym only when the boys were through with it; and we had a grand total of about 30 spectators at all our games combined. Our principal did not announce any of our games, and did not provide a late bus so that the kids could stay and watch. One time I asked if it would be possible to get uniforms for our team. I was told to earn the money through car washes, dances, and bake sales. Yet each of the boys received a brand new $30 uniform this year.

Everyone seems to think that girls playing basketball is a big joke, but I am dead serious. If we are good enough to be called varsity, aren't we good enough to be respected?

—Jane L."

travel and play the best teams just as our men do, we wouldn't have won the championship.[42]

The ERA—Optimism at the Start

But with all the gains women made during the 1970s, there was one major disappointment. The Equal Rights Amendment, or ERA, had first been proposed to Congress back in 1923, by the efforts of the National Woman's Party. The amendment would make it illegal to deny or limit people's rights because of their sex.

The ERA had been proposed in each session of Congress since 1923, but was voted down every year. In 1972, largely because of pressure from women's groups such as NOW, the Equal Rights Amendment passed both houses of Congress. The battle was not won, however, until three-fourths of the states ratified the amendment in their legislatures.

The wording of the 1972 amendment was short and simple: "Equality of rights under the law shall not be denied or abridged by the United States or by any state on account of sex." Even so, quipped columnist Erma Bombeck, "Twenty-four words have never been so misunderstood since the four words 'One size fits all.'"[43]

States' ratification of the ERA seemed like a sure thing in 1972. But after being ratified rather quickly in thirty-three states, the amendment soon became bogged down in political stand-offs at the state level. The amendment by law had to be ratified by thirty-eight states by the deadline of March 1979. It had not received the necessary votes by that time, however, so Congress granted an additional thirty-nine months for the undecided states to vote on the bill.

"American Women Have Never Had It So Good"

The ERA had strong opponents. Many people believed it was un-necessary because women were al-ready protected under the Constitution and the Bill of Rights. Conservative religious groups crit-icized women's rights advocates for undermining the family struc-ture which they felt was the bed-rock of the American way of life. "God Almighty created men and women biologically different and with differing needs and roles," proclaimed the Reverend Jerry Falwell. "Good hus-bands who are godly men are good

leaders. Their wives and children want to follow them."[44]

One of the most outspoken critics of the ERA was a conservative Repub-lican with a master's degree in govern-ment from Radcliffe named Phyllis Schlafly. She founded an antifeminist group called the Eagle Forum, whose purpose was to work against states' ratification of the ERA. Like Falwell

Phyllis Schlafly, founder of the Eagle Forum, an antifeminist organization, speaks with reporters during a 1975 "Stop the Equal Rights Amendment" rally at the Illinois State Capitol.

and others, she believed the bill was potentially dangerous, and warned that if it passed, women would be drafted into the army. In addition, men would no longer be required to provide for their wives and children.

Schlafly scoffed at the notion that women were discriminated against in American society. Calling feminists "a bunch of military radicals," she argued that women were treated very well:

> The claim that American women are downtrodden and unfairly treated is the fraud of the century. The truth is that American women have never had it so good. Why should we lower ourselves to "equal rights" when we already have the status of special privilege?[45]

By June 30, 1982, only thirty-five states had ratified the ERA, and the bill died. Many historians say that while the extra time did not help the ERA, it gave antifeminist groups like Phyllis Schlafly's the opportunity to organize strong and effective opposition. The momentum of the women's movement, which had built to such a strong peak during the '70s and had resulted in great strides for women's equality, suddenly languished as the decade ended.

Chapter Three

Native Americans gather at the capital in 1978 to protest government violation of their rights. In the 1970s, many ethnic and racial groups tried to obtain an equal share of political and economic rights.

A Piece of the Pie

The 1960s, especially the early part of the decade, had been a time of great progress for black Americans. After the 1954 Supreme Court decision in *Brown v. Board of Education,* which established that segregated public schools were unconstitutional, civil rights leaders were optimistic.

Such optimism was well founded—sit-ins, freedom rides, and solidarity marches to places like Birmingham and Selma, Alabama, and even Washington,

D.C., had resulted in civil rights legislation. Several black mayors had been elected in large U.S. cities. Too, more black students than ever before were finishing high school and going on to college.

But the late 1960s saw a halt to the optimism. Black Americans still had many grievances, but they weren't being solved or addressed as quickly as they were in the early '60s. Besides this, black radicals such as H. Rap Brown and

Stokely Carmichael condemned the slow progress of working within the white system. They called for more militant methods of achieving black power. Such rhetoric, writes one historian, "soon aroused a festering anger that had slept uneasily in the squalor of American cities. Shouting 'Burn, baby, burn,' ghetto blacks ignited a series of violent upheavals that spread from Harlem to Watts to Newark and Detroit."[46]

"Toward Two Societies, One Black, One White"

By the beginning of the 1970s, the status of civil rights in America was at a new low. Black Americans were without the conciliatory leadership of Martin Luther King Jr., who had been murdered in 1968. Many white Americans who had worked alongside blacks during earlier civil rights efforts were less supportive now, fearful that the violence in the cities would spill into their neighborhoods.

Many historians agree that President Richard Nixon's lack of interest in racial issues did much to worsen the strife in the black communities. During his campaign for the 1968 election, he had largely ignored black voters—pragmatic politically, since blacks rarely voted Republican. Instead, he had tried to win over voters in the South who, although they usually voted Democratic, were unhappy with the civil rights legislation that had been passed in recent years.

To appeal to these conservative voters, Nixon was openly critical of the more liberal policies of his predecessor, Lyndon Johnson. And while the President's Advisory Commission on Civil Disorders had warned that the United States was quickly moving "toward two societies, one black, one white—separate and unequal,"[47] Nixon's administration made no specific promises to black Americans.

COINTELPRO

One of the campaign promises Nixon *had* made that related to civil rights was to get rid of those he termed "troublemakers"—radical groups, especially black militant organizations like the Black Liberation Front and the Black Panthers. FBI director J. Edgar Hoover considered the Panthers the single greatest threat to the security of the United States.

Nixon's plan for "getting rid of the troublemakers" involved huge increases in budget for the Justice Department's Law Enforcement Assistance Administration, whose purpose was to prepare for armed uprising by militant groups. The budget for this department was $63 million in 1969, and increased to $268 million in 1970. By 1972, the

The Black Panthers, a radical black rights group, march in the streets in a show of black power. During the 1970s, such radical groups stopped advocating violent means to achieve their goals.

budget had ballooned to $700 million! The funds were used to buy crowd control equipment, weapons, and even armored cars with which to transport large groups of prisoners.

In addition, the FBI stepped up COINTELPRO—the code name for its Counter Intelligence Program. COINTELPRO carried out electronic surveillance of black dissidents by tapping phones and secretly recording conversations that would help federal officials arrest and imprison those thought to be dangerous.

The FBI waged war against black militants in more devious ways, too:

FBI agents also used fake press releases to spread false rumors about social activists; hired undercover agents to commit crimes in the name of the more militant black power movements; violently attacked competing organizations; and created an atmosphere of tension, confusion, and division within the organizations under surveillance.[48]

By 1972 most black militant organizations like the Black Panthers had decreased their activity in the black communities. Almost a thousand "troublemakers" had been imprisoned, and those who were left were reluctant to continue the struggle in the same way. "We've rejected the rhetoric of the gun," explained one. "It got about 40 of us killed and sent hundreds of us to prison. Our goal is to organize the black communities politically."[49]

Busing and Racial Balance

One issue that troubled many black leaders was the continuance of segregation in America's public schools. Although the Supreme Court had banned segregated schools as unconstitutional, they were as segregated in the early 1970s as they had ever been. Approximately 82 percent of black students attended black majority schools.

Ironically, however, the southern schools were not at fault, as they had been in years past. Those schools had been segregated because of rules and laws in the South against integration.

The segregation that was rampant throughout northern cities was voluntary: Districts were laid out along neighborhood lines, and blacks and whites tended to reside in different neighborhoods.

But whatever the reason for the segregation, argued black leaders, it still existed. It meant that integration, which was the law, was not occurring as intended. The only way to achieve integration in schools was to bus whites to predominantly black schools and blacks to predominantly white schools. However, the plan caused outbreaks of violence in cities like Boston and Louisville.

Buses carrying black students were stoned, mobs of angry white parents carrying signs with racial slurs blocked driveways and entrances to schools. Many schools had to be closed temporarily when officials worried that some students might be injured or killed.

As one black woman who had been a student in 1974 in Boston recalls,

It was hard to learn anything. . . . At least twice a week we had an early dismissal; they brought us out the side door any time there was a disturbance. The buses were stoned every other day. They shouted, "Niggahs! We're going to burn you!"[50]

Decoy on the Buses

Police stand guard as black students arrive at Boston High School in 1974. The students were met with violent white mobs who protested their presence.

During the height of the racial tension in Boston in 1974 as students were being bused to achieve racial balance, school officials at South Boston High found themselves in a potentially dangerous situation. With white mobs outside and black students inside, they decided to use a busload of black adults as a decoy, so that the students could be sent home without being hurt by the mobs. In her book Struggle and Love 1972–1997: From the Gary Convention to the Aftermath of the Million Man March, *author Mary Hull quotes one of the women on the decoy bus as she describes the experience.*

"So we got on the bus and we tried to joke. We were lying on the floor. Percy Wilson, who was head of [the Roxbury] Multi-Services Center said, 'Oh, God, I thought I left these days in Mississippi. I didn't think I would be in this kind of situation again.' But we were nervous. . . . We came around the front part of the building where the people, the mob—in a sense, crazy mob—was and they could see us. We were slouching so we would look like students. . . . And while we were trying to distract them, hopefully distracting them, the two buses with the students would take another route and get down the hill.

When we started down that hill, I tell you, they rushed past the police and started rocking those buses. I know they rocked the one I was on. And as we were going down, they started throwing everything they could get in their hands. Not rocks, they looked like boulders. . . . And when we got down the hill, it was complete silence on the bus. And I think a lot of us just started crying. Fear and anger and hurt."

"It's Nation Time!"

School integration was one of several areas that frustrated black Americans in the 1970s. Many believed that the lack of strong leadership in the black community was a factor that made resolution of such issues difficult.

The lack of strength came in part from the two different schools of thought among blacks. Some were integrationists—those who believed as did Martin Luther King Jr., that blacks and whites needed to eliminate the differences between themselves. Others were nationalists, who believed it was more important to retain their differences as black Americans. Malcolm X, who was murdered in 1965, was a black nationalist.

Both men had believed in the same goals, however, even acknowledging that working together would be more effective than working separately. In that spirit, more than eight thousand black Americans came together in March 1972 in Gary, Indiana, for the first convention of the National Black Political

To protest court-ordered desegregation in the Boston schools, a demonstrator carries an effigy of a black person that carries the message, "go home."

Assembly. Their purpose was to listen to one another, to try to find common ground.

One of the most dynamic speakers was Jesse Jackson, a former colleague of King. In his speech before the delegates, Jackson expressed the frustration many blacks felt at being left out of the U.S. political process:

> We are pregnant! We are ready for change, and whether a doctor is there or not, the water has broke, the blood has spilled—a new black baby is gonna be born! . . . No more bowing and scraping! We are 25 million strong. Cut us in or cut us out![51]

Jesse Jackson, a colleague of Reverend Martin Luther King, organized efforts to get blacks registered and to the voting booth.

And when Jackson asked the crowd, "What time is it?" the answer was loud and clear: "It's Nation Time!"[52]

Mayor Richard Hatcher of Gary had predicted at the convention that "The Seventies will be the decade of an independent black political thrust. Its destiny depends upon us here at Gary."[53] His optimism was perhaps idealistic, but not entirely unfounded.

Although divisiveness existed in black leadership, and no one leader emerged to unify the various groups, historians say there was a tremendous birth of interest in becoming involved in the political process. In huge numbers, blacks registered to vote; black candidates appeared on ballots on the county, state, and national levels.

The Poorest Minority

Black Americans were not the only minority who believed more action was needed to secure their rights. Native Americans also began to demand civil rights in 1969. At that time, the average Native American family earned less than $1,800 a year—more than $4,200 less than the national average. And while only about 5 percent of the nation's workers were unemployed, 39 percent of Native Americans were out of work. Housing on reservations was substandard, drinking and drug use was rampant, and depression and suicide among Native Americans was soaring.

Native Americans accused the U.S. government of mistreating and exploiting them, as well as of stealing their land. On November 20, 1969, representatives of twenty Native American tribes reclaimed Alcatraz Island (vacant since the federal prison there closed in 1963). One leader of the occupation, LaNada Means, explained that their action

> was symbolic of telling the American Government and American people that they are not going to continue to steal our land nor are they going to tell us what to do. . . . [Alcatraz] was symbolic in

Reverse Racism?

To counter the effects of job discrimination, a technique known as "affirmative action" has been used. It includes special efforts to hire members of minority groups such as blacks, women, and handicapped people. Policies of affirmative action were praised by black leaders in the 1970s for giving black people expanded opportunites for college and jobs.

However, there was a great deal of criticism, especially by white males, who felt that they were being reversely discriminated against when colleges and employers used affirmative action policies. California was the setting of an important court ruling in 1978.

The debate began when Allan Bakke, a white engineer in his thirties, applied to the University of California at Davis Medical School. He was turned down by U.C. Davis, as well as by eleven other medical schools. Bakke disagreed with U.C. Davis's affirmative action policy of reserving sixteen of the one hundred places in its entering class for disadvantaged students—blacks, Hispanics, and Asians.

Bakke claimed in his lawsuit that he was more qualified than some of those sixteen students, and therefore he was the victim of reverse discrimination. The California Supreme Court ruled in his favor, and the University appealed to the U.S. Supreme Court. Archibald Cox, the lawyer for the university, argued that race should be a factor in selecting qualified applicants, since for generations, racial discrimination had denied minority students access to such opportunities.

The Supreme Court disagreed in a 5-4 decision, finding instead that Bakke should be admitted to the university and that U.C. Davis's affirmative action policy *was* the equivalent of reverse discrimination. In his book *Into the Fire: African Americans Since 1970*, Robin D. G. Kelley quotes one of the dissenting justices who felt the Bakke decision was a tragedy. Thurgood Marshall, the first black justice to serve on the Supreme Court wrote, "The dream of America as a great melting pot has not been realized for the Negro; because of his skin color, he never even made it into the pot."

reawakening Indian consciousness and bringing attention to Indian people."[54]

Because the island was deserted, U.S. officials allowed the occupation for eighteen months before marshals removed the last people from Alcatraz in June 1971.

Apples, Uncle Tomahawks, and Wounded Knee

Just as black Americans differed in their ideas of how to achieve political and economic goals, Native American groups also were of different minds as to how they wished to accomplish their goals. Many wanted to refrain from confrontation. They worried that such actions as the Alcatraz occupation would cause government officials to be more strict with Native American people.

On the other hand, many agreed with the leaders of the activists of the American Indian Movement (AIM), who urged Native Americans to be more assertive in their demands, resorting to violence as a political tool. They laughingly called more conservative Native Americans "Uncle Tomahawks" or "apples," people who were red on the outside but white on the inside. The time for waiting patiently, they said, was long past.

The most daring action took place on February 27, 1973, on the site of the U.S. Army massacre of three hundred Sioux in 1890. More than two hundred members of AIM took over the village of Wounded Knee, South Dakota, on the Oglala Sioux Reservation. The militants demanded a renegotiation of various treaties the government had made with Native Americans. Hundreds of law enforcement officers—FBI, U.S. marshals, and National Guard—surrounded the village.

The occupation lasted seventy-one days and resulted in the deaths of two Native Americans. It was also, say experts Paul Chaat Smith and Robert Allen Warrior, "the final performance of AIM's daring brand of political theater."[55] Although the drama at Wounded Knee called attention to a minority that had gotten little publicity up until then, the demands of the AIM leaders were not met. Three hundred Native American people, were arrested at Wounded Knee. And afterward, divisiveness among the movement resulted in poor organization and bickering among its leaders.

Success in the Courts

While activism among Native Americans was not effective in the 1970s, litigation was. Some of the court cases involved claims to land, on the

Demands at Wounded Knee

During the occupation of Wounded Knee in South Dakota on February 27, 1973, members of the American Indian Movement issued a list of demands that was given to Justice Department officials. These demands were reprinted in Paul Chaat Smith's and Robert Allen Warrior's Like a Hurricane: The Indian Movement from Alcatraz to Wounded Knee.

Members of the radical Native American group AIM camp out at Wounded Knee in 1973 in hopes of gaining greater land rights from the U.S. government.

"DEMANDS:

I. Senator William Fulbright to convene Senate Foreign Relations Committee immediately for hearings on treaties made with American Indian Nations and ratified by the Congress of the U.S.

II. Senator Edward Kennedy to convene Senate Sub-Committee on Administrative Practices and Procedures for immediate, full-scale investigations and exposure of the Bureau of Indian Affairs and the Department of the Interior from the Agency, reservation offices, to the area offices, to the central office in Washington, D.C.

III. Senator James Abourezk to convene the Senate Sub-Committee on Indian Affairs for a complete investigation of all Sioux Reservations in South Dakota.

People we will negotiate with:

1. Mr. Ehrlichman of the White House,

2. Senators Kennedy, Abourezk, and Fulbright—or their top aides,

3. The Commissioner of the BIA and the Secretary of the Interior.

The only two options open to the United States of America are:

1. They wipe out the old people, women, children, and men, by shooting and attacking us.

2. They negotiate our demands.

Signed:

Oglala Sioux Civil Rights Organization"

The assistant attorney general (in car) of South Dakota is escorted out of Wounded Knee by members of AIM after attempting to negotiate terms with the Native Americans camped there in protest.

grounds that historic treaties were illegal. In several cases, Native Americans won vast sums of money or land. The Passamaquoddy and Penobscot tribes, for example, sued to recover 12.5 million acres of land in Maine—nearly two-thirds of the state. They settled instead for $81 million, which allowed these tribes to start businesses and increase their living standard.

Some of the court cases focused on the exploitation of Native Americans by the U.S. government. During the energy shortages of the 1970s, for instance, great pressure was placed on Native Americans to allow increased mining and drilling on their land. (Nearly half of U.S. uranium reserves, as well as huge deposits of coal and natural gas, lie on Indian-owned land.)

However, Native American activists were more outspoken than they ever had been. "We want to contribute to meeting America's goals of energy independence," said one Navajo leader. "But America will not be permitted to march to that goal as it marched to the Pacific—over the backs of this country's native peoples."[56]

The courts agreed, granting various Native Americans the right to negotiate their own contracts for energy companies that wanted to drill on

their lands. These leases allowed tribes to collect higher cash returns and create many jobs for Native Americans.

"The Longest Walk"

Native Americans also spoke up about abuses to their lands that, in some cases, caused tribal leaders to refuse drilling or digging rights to energy companies. Some excavations would disturb sacred burial grounds. As one tribal leader insisted, "The coal can just stay where it is until they find a way to get it out without wrecking everything else."[57]

However, in other instances, Native American leaders were concerned

Native Americans protest in front of the FBI building. Native American protests resulted in increased rights over reservation lands.

about the pollution caused by uranium mining or the coal-burning power plants on their land. "My sheep are dying," one woman cried. "Their noses bleed. The baby goats do not grow up. . . . This is the biggest, baddest disease ever visited on mankind."[58]

Native American leaders called national attention to their plight in 1978. In a peaceful demonstration, activists from various tribes spent five months walking three-thousand miles from San Francisco to Washington, D.C. The Longest Walk, as it was called, was a show of strength for Native Americans. As activist Clyde Bellecourt stated, "We are here to let America know that everything hasn't been given away, that everything hasn't been stolen from us, that we are still a way of life that survives."[59]

As the decade ended, the movements of black and Native Americans were in different stages. Native Americans had gained public attention to their cause, as black Americans had done in the 1960s. In comparison, the difficulties of implementing hard-won changes for black Americans proved a sobering task.

Chapter Four

In celebration of Earth Day in 1970, protesters both plant flowers and carry signs to remind people of the dangers of pollution. The public gained a greater appreciation of the environment during the 1970s.

Energy and the Environment

Rachel Carson's 1962 best-seller *Silent Spring* alerted people to the dangers of pesticides in the environment. "As man proceeds toward his announced goal of the conquest of nature," she wrote, "he has written a depressing record of destruction, directed not only against the earth he inhabits, but against the life that shares it with him."[60]

The images she shared of a world where rivers and lakes are dead, where birds and fish have been poisoned, served as a wake-up call to an American public that had never really thought about the effects of chemicals on the environment. Because of Rachel Carson, people in the 1960s began to take a widespread interest in maintaining the environment.

Naive at First

In the years following the release of *Silent Spring*, a groundswell of support for legislation developed to regulate pollution, although as one expert writes, Congress's response was "slow and piecemeal . . . and extremely gingerly where large economic interests were concerned."[61] Even so, new laws that protected drinking water and established smokestack standards were good beginnings.

Many young people who had joined in the civil rights and antiwar protests of the 1960s became the base of the new environmental movement. They were anxious to make a difference, say historians, but naive. At the time, no one was aware of the extent of damage to the earth; Americans believed that it was just a matter of a few well-placed laws, and things would improve. As one writer explains,

> The earth wasn't beyond repair: it was sort of like a basement rec room filled with partying teenagers

The Rise of Greenpeace

The 1970s saw the rise of a number of environmental organizations, and increased membership in those that had been around for years, such as the Audubon Society and the Sierra Club. One of the most publicized of these new organizations was Greenpeace, which became known for its confrontational style of promoting its ideas.

Greenpeace was begun by a group of Sierra Club members who were disappointed in the club's refusal to take a stronger stand against U.S. nuclear testing in the Pacific Ocean. Hoping they could stop the tests—or at least call national attention to them—they hired a boat and tried to sail into the testing site off the shore of Alaska. Although they were forced back by stormy seas, they did catch the attention of the international media.

One of Greenpeace's chief causes was that of whales, which were being killed in such huge numbers that several species were in danger of extinction. In 1975 they began a campaign against Soviet and Japanese whaling vessels by positioning their small boat between the whale and the hunters. Occasionally they successfully impeded the hunters, but more often they were only able to document the carnage. The films Greenpeace photographers took of the bloody killings were circulated around the world; as a result more and more people understood that it was important to "Save the Whales."

The same confrontational methods were used in 1976 when the fur of baby harp seals became a hot commodity. Every spring thousands of young seals were clubbed to death by fur trappers. Greenpeace crews traveled to the northernmost coasts of Canada and sprayed an indelible (but harmless) dye on the babies, making their pelts worthless to the trappers.

who throw cigarette butts on the floor, nick the wood paneling, and crank the volume up to ten. . . . It wasn't large corporations dumping dioxins into the water supply, it was *you*: that tinfoil gum wrapper, that pop-top, that cigarette butt you dropped.[62]

Earth Day

In the spirit of "rolling up our sleeves and getting to work," an event called Earth Day took place on April 22, 1970. The idea was suggested by Senator Gaylord Nelson of Wisconsin in a speech made the year before. He suggested that American schools and universities take a day to educate themselves about the earth, in the same spirit of the "teach-ins" of the antiwar movement in the 1960s.

The idea received a huge response. More than twelve thousand high schools and colleges around the country suspended classes for a day; and thousands more elementary schools turned youngsters loose to pick up litter around neighborhoods. Hundreds of thousands gathered on Fifth Avenue in New York and on Capitol Mall

During the first Earth Day in 1970, a gas mask–wearing protester joins thousands of people gathered in New York to show support for a cleaner environment.

in Washington, D.C., to show support for the new concern for the environment and to protest against abuse of land, air, water, and wildlife. *Time* magazine estimated that thirty million Americans participated in the event in some way.

For politicians, the event was easy to support, for it was not controversial like the Vietnam War rallies and protests that were common at the time. As environmental experts Marc Mowrey and Tim Redmond recall,

Both houses of Congress . . . decided to adjourn for the day, since so many members were going to be making Earth Day appearances. Mayors, governors, aldermen, city council members, and village trustees, from Florida to Alaska, from southern California to northern Maine, had agreed to march in parades and make speeches.[63]

Limits of Government Commitment

Although politicians indicated their support for the environment on Earth Day, environmental experts were disappointed. Few of the millions who participated seemed to understand the enormous change necessary in reversing the earth-unfriendly direction America was going in. Some tried to point out that it was the country's very lifestyle that was at fault, not just a few factories or litterers.

Environmental activist Denis Hayes chastised American society in 1970—a society which, he explained, accounted for only six percent of the earth's population, but which consumed half of the world's raw materials. And the corporations that fostered such consumption bore much of the blame:

I suspect that politicians and businessmen who are jumping on the environmental bandwagon don't have the slightest idea what they are getting into. They are talking about filters on smokestacks while we are challenging corporate irresponsibility. . . . You simply can't live an ecologically sound life in America. That is not one of the options that is open to you.[64]

Even if there had been more understanding by the American people about what true environmentalism entailed, however, the Nixon administration was not supportive. Within days of Earth Day, Secretary of the Interior Walter Hickle announced approval of the eight-hundred-mile Alaska pipeline, which many considered a dangerous threat to the wildlife and water supply. In addition, environmentalists were also alarmed at the news that, while agreeing to ban the use of the pesticide DDT, Nixon was allowing American chemical plants to export it for use by food producers in other countries—much of whose produce ended up in American supermarkets.

But perhaps the most alarming example of the administration's attitude toward the environment was the president's support of the new supersonic transport (SST). Experts warned that the aircraft could destroy the ozone layer, thus making people vulnerable to radiation. Too, environmental scientists predicted the SST would release large amounts of water vapor, carbon dioxide, nitrogen oxides, and other materials into the atmosphere, which would have an adverse warming effect on the earth.

With Nixon's hearty approval, the vote went to Congress, which voted down the SST in May 1971. The president was very disappointed. "America must and will continue pushing outward the horizons of the unknown," he said. "We may have lost this one, but we're going to win the next one."[65]

In the early 1970s, environmentalists were far more interested in conservation of wildlife than of another of earth's resources—energy. However, late in the autumn of 1973, energy—or the lack of it—grabbed headlines as never before.

Out of Gas

The United States had been spoiled, for energy had been cheap and abundant since the 1950s. American oil wells had been gushing away, producing far more than the country could use. But as the years went by, the country could use

plenty. In 1960, the United States was using 9.7 million barrels a day; by 1970, the figure had increased to 16.2 million. And when the energy shortage hit, Americans were using 16.8 million barrels of oil per day, including at least two million barrels imported from overseas.

The trouble was not a shortage worldwide, for the Arab-dominated Organization of Petroleum Exporting Countries (OPEC) were producing as much as ever. However, the Arab countries were fighting a war with Israel, and because the United States was supplying aid and weapons to Israel, these nations wanted to punish the United States by cutting off its oil shipments.

"A Problem We Must All Face Together"

On November 8, 1973, President Nixon addressed the American people on television. "I want to talk to you about a serious national problem," he said, "a problem we must all face together in the months and years ahead. We are heading toward the most acute shortage of energy since World War II."[66]

He went on to explain new emergency policies that would help America through the oil shortage. Thermostat temperatures would be lowered to sixty-eight degrees, and air travel would be cut by 10 percent. Highway speed limits would be lowered to fifty-five miles per hour in an attempt to conserve gasoline. Daylight saving time would be extended into the winter, and factories would work shorter shifts.

The rudest jolt to the American consumer, however, was the closing of gas stations on Sunday, and the rationing of fuel implemented by several states. Gas stations were easy to spot. They were the places with long lines of cars snaking for miles, with exasperated

During the Energy Crisis

During the energy crisis of 1973, President Nixon ordered that the clocks not be turned back an hour in late October as they usually were. Instead, the United States would remain on the summer's daylight saving time in order to save energy. In her book Platforms: A Microwaved Cultural Chronicle of the 1970s, *Pagan Kennedy recalls her feelings of getting ready for school in what felt like the middle of the night.*

"So the winter of the energy crisis, kids went to school in mornings that were like nighttime. When I woke up at 6:30, it was really 5:30 in the morning (non-1973 time). And when my family sat around the table for breakfast, it seemed more like we were eating a midnight snack. All of the lights in the kitchen blazed and the windows, like black mirrors, reflected us in ghostly shapes. I used to imagine that the world outside had turned to tar, like some 'Twilight Zone' episode where we were the last ones left on Earth, only we didn't know it yet. I cannot exactly express it, the horror of those black-windowed breakfasts. Here my parents were—my mother telling us to finish our oatmeal and my father

reading the paper—as if they were trying to trick my sister and me into thinking everything was normal, that the sun was out instead of the stars.

At 7:30 (really 6:30—I was always subtracting an hour in my head), I walked the two blocks to my bus stop. When my mother hugged me goodbye, I could feel by the tightness of her grip how afraid she was to have me stand under the stars, alone, waiting for the bus. She made me carry a flashlight, which I clicked off as soon as she closed the door. I'd walk along between the pools of light cast by the streetlamps, which made the pavement scintillate with each of my steps. It was magical and scary. My mother had told me not to talk to any strangers in the dark, and I half expected some man to follow me or watch me from the shadows, but no one ever did.

When the bus came, it bore down on me with its headlights, groaned, and then swung open its hinged door to let me in. It would carry me to my day of hiding in the corner of the classroom. It would carry me to this senseless new school that existed inside this senseless world of oil rations, Watergate, and Vietnam."

In 1979, cars line up early at a Los Angeles service station to obtain gas. During the fuel crisis, gas stations enforced odd/even gas rationing—motorists could only buy gas on certain days.

drivers fighting—and sometimes even shooting one another—as the waits sometimes took several hours.

"These People Are Like Animals"

The frustration was often turned on the station owners themselves, who frequently had to put up "No Gas" signs as the heavy demand emptied their supplies. One Texaco attendant said,

These people are like animals foraging for food. If you can't give them gas, they'll threaten to beat you up, wreck your station, run you over with a car. We're all so busy at the pumps that somebody walked in and stole my adding machine and the leukemia-fund can.[67]

Some sensed that the nation was frustrated in a way it had never been before. Wrote one observer,

The sudden scramble for what had once been so plentiful and cheap, seemed like a symbol of America's mediocrity, its transformation into a country that could be pinched by other world powers and circumscribed by scarcity.[68]

There were also mixed answers to the question: Whose fault is it? Some blamed OPEC, others the government. And the notion that the whole shortage was a conspiracy cooked up by the oil companies to increase demand and hike prices was common, too.

Project Independence

During the embargo, Nixon proposed that the best solution to future trouble would be to completely eliminate American dependence on foreign oil. Speaking to the nation, Nixon suggested "an endeavor that in this Bicentennial Era we can appropriately call Project Independence."[69]

Nixon was confident, he said, that the same American ingenuity that had put a man on the moon in 1969 could certainly find other sources of energy for American industry and homes. In addition to finding new oil reserves in the United States—including the oil that would come via the Alaska pipeline—he asked for more concentration on the use of coal and the de-

velopment of other sources of power, such as solar, geomass, shale, and nuclear energy. The goal would be energy self-sufficiency by 1980.

Project Independence was soundly criticized by many environmentalists. Some protested that instead of finding new sources of energy, America should be addressing the overuse and waste of energy at the industrial level. Others worried that the strides that had been made in environmental legislation would be wiped out by the pollution caused by additional coal mining.

"He is really calling for massive strip-mining for coal," said one Sierra Club official, "and massive destruction of the land and pollution of the land and water."[70]

"We Can't Live in a Garden of Eden"

Project Independence was unsuccessful, for by the time the energy crisis ended in March 1974, Americans were more dependent on foreign oil than ever. That dependence grew as the decade went on. Part of the reason was the large increase in technology that called for more factories and more industry. In addition, the alternative forms of energy Nixon had encouraged were more expensive than originally thought. Even coal mining proved undesirable, for new information about the health hazards of coal dust for miners and damage to the environment made more reliance on coal reserves unacceptable.

Nuclear energy was the one avenue about which Nixon and his advisors continued to be optimistic. In the early 1970s, several nuclear reactors were already in operation, but their efficiency was questionable. One reactor in Vermont, for example, was shut down seventeen times during a nineteen-month period during the oil embargo because it was not working properly.

The American public was nervous about nuclear power in the 1970s. Anything "nuclear" sounded too much like a bomb, and the possibility of radioactive fallout was always a worry. But in 1973 the government scoffed at such concern, claiming that the odds of a reactor accident were equivalent to the odds of getting hit by a meteor—about once every million years.

"We can't live in a Garden of Eden," said one head of the Atomic Energy Commission, "and still have a technological society." [71] President Nixon wholeheartedly agreed, although admitting that "all this business about breeder reactors and nuclear power is over my head." [72] He maintained that it was important to accelerate the building of new reactors and suggested that the elaborate safety measures required caused unreasonable costs and delays.

"I am not afraid," he maintained, "not because I know much about it, but because what I do know tells me that here we have a new source of energy." [73]

Three Mile Island

On March 28, 1979, however, the worst fears of the American people were realized when an accident occurred at 4:00 A.M. at Pennsylvania's Three Mile Island nuclear power plant. A combination of human and mechanical failure resulted in a breakdown of the reactor's cooling system. More than 830 liters of coolant water were drained from the reactor, and the floor of the containment building was flooded. One writer noted,

> The training and written emergency procedures of the operators in the [Three Mile Island] control room had never dealt with the possibility of an accident in which coolant was lost . . . so that the operators repeatedly misunderstood what was happening. [74]

Technicians worked feverishly to avoid a meltdown of the core, which would have resulted in the release of dangerous amounts of radioactive isotopes into the area surrounding the plant.

At first it seemed to experts that real danger had been avoided. Local

Mothers and children play in the shadow of the Three Mile Island nuclear plant.

By Friday, March 30, however, the optimism had vanished. A hydrogen bubble had formed inside the reactor, and workers were nervous that if the bubble expanded, the entire reactor might explode. Such an explosion would almost certainly result in injuries and deaths in the tens of thousands.

Pennsylvania's governor Richard Thornburgh quietly ordered experts to devise a plan to evacuate a million people, while in the meantime urged pregnant women and young children living near the plant to leave the area. On the network news that evening, Walter Cronkite told viewers, "The world has never known a day quite like today. It faced the considerable uncertainties and dangers of the worst nuclear power plant accident of the atomic age. And the horror tonight is that it could get much worse."[75]

"Not All the Safety Assurances in the World"

radio and television stations assured people that the accident was over, and there was no cause for panic or alarm.

More than one hundred thousand people fled their homes, but it proved unnecessary. Workers found a way to shrink the gas bubble, and the cooling of the reactor continued. Within a few days, the crisis was over, and life returned to normal for the people around Three Mile Island.

The accident resulted in no deaths or injuries, although it did heighten Americans' fear. Experts had promised that nuclear power would be cheap and safe, but it was neither of those. The Three Mile Island plant would never reopen, and the cost of the cleanup, which took more than ten years, was over a billion dollars.

As for the safety of nuclear energy, the assurances of nuclear-power advocates meant nothing in the wake of the near miss of Three Mile Island. The following years brought increased public pressure to shut down existing plants, and to end plans to build new ones. As Governor Thornburgh explained, "Not all the safety assurances in the world can erase the awareness of these good people that something out there is powerful and strange and not entirely under control." [76]

Love Canal

Governor Thornburgh's words might also have referred to another of the decade's wor-

ries—toxic waste. In the 1970s waste from industry and agriculture was often disposed of carelessly—dumped into rivers or buried in landfills. Most of the sites used for disposing of hazardous waste were not maintained to keep the material from contaminating the soil, water, or air. And occasionally hazardous waste dumped years before surfaced in communities where people were completely unaware of its presence.

Love Canal, in a suburban area of Niagara Falls, New York, was just such a community. The canal was dug by a nineteenth-century developer named William Love, who intended it

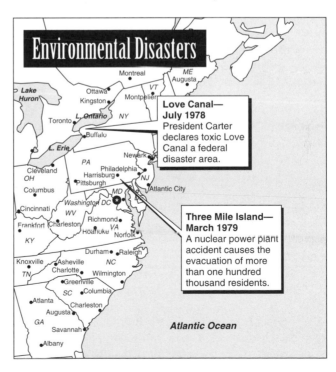

Environmental Disasters

Love Canal—
July 1978
President Carter declares toxic Love Canal a federal disaster area.

Three Mile Island—
March 1979
A nuclear power plant accident causes the evacuation of more than one hundred thousand residents.

Atlantic Ocean

Mysterious Ailments Near Love Canal

In their book Not in Our Backyard: The People and Events That Shaped America's Modern Environmental Movement, *authors Marc Mowrey and Tim Redmond recount some of the early warnings one young mother had that her neighborhood, Love Canal, was actually the site of illegally dumped toxic chemicals.*

"Michael Gibb started kindergarten at the same school [under which chemicals had been dumped] in September 1977. After a few weeks, he started having health problems. He developed rashes, and his face would swell up. His eyes always seemed to hurt. Lois and Harry were concerned, but not overly worried: children were prone to all kinds of bugs, rashes, and allergies.

In December, Michael began having seizures, and the doctor diagnosed him as having epilepsy. Two months later, his white blood cell count suddenly began dropping. Lois took him to the doctor frequently, sometimes several times a month, but nothing the doctor did would make the problems go away. It didn't make any sense—Michael had always been a healthy kid.

For more than a year a *Niagara Gazette* reporter named Michael Brown had been writing stories about hazardous chemicals leaking out of an old dump site, but Gibbs had never paid attention. She always assumed it was on the other side of town.

In April, though, Lois learned from one of Brown's stories that the Ninety-ninth Street school where Michael attended kindergarten was built right on top of the old chemical dump. She'd

A man and his dog sit below a handmade sign sarcastically advertising the sale of chemicals that have seeped into the basement of his home in Love Canal, New York.

started watching the paper for developments—and the article in today's edition scared her half to death. One by one, Brown listed the chemicals that he suspected were present in the dump. One by one, he described the health problems they were known to cause. And one by one, Lois Gibbs recognized her son's mysterious symptoms."

to generate electricity for a community he planned to build. The community was never built, and the property was sold to the Hooker Chemical Company as a dumping ground for its waste materials.

The canal was filled by the early 1950s and was covered over with dirt. And when the Niagara Falls Board of Education wanted a place to build a new elementary school in the rapidly-growing neighborhood, Hooker sold the site for a dollar.

A young boy sits outside the fenced-off area that marks the contaminated neighborhood of Love Canal, New York.

But by the late 1970s, it became clear to the residents of Love Canal that something was very wrong. Children were getting sick far more often than children in other neighborhoods. Incidents of cancer among residents was far higher than the national average, as were miscarriages and stillbirths.

A Federal Disaster Area

There were other signs, too. The air had a foul smell, and the trees were black. Every once in a while dark sludge oozed out of the ground or through a resident's basement wall. The cause, it was discovered, was 42 million pounds of pesticides and poisonous chemicals, including the deadly poison called dioxin, or TCDD. So toxic is TCDD, in fact, that it would take only three ounces to kill the entire population of New York City—and Love Canal had been the site of more than 450 pounds of it!

As environmentalists, chemists, and medical researchers agreed that the area would have to be vacated, residents panicked. They could not live in their homes any longer, and they certainly couldn't sell them. It would take many thousands of dollars to move to another neighborhood; what were they to do?

In July 1978, President Carter declared Love Canal a federal disaster area, and earmarked $15 million to relocate the families. And although the incident had been resolved for the residents, it left the American public uneasy. How many more Love Canals were there? Experts admitted that it was almost impossible to know, but that it was likely that Love Canal was not an isolated incident.

As the decade drew to a close, many people were beginning to realize that irreversible destruction of the earth was possible. The potential of catastrophes, whether from a nuclear accident or thoughtless disposal of poison, was a sobering thought—one that would not go away.

Chapter Five

*In a publicity stunt, a local department store asked "real people"
to model the latest fashion, hot pants. Hot pants were just one of
the fads of the 1970s.*

"No Rules" Rule: Fashion and Fads in the Seventies

The fashion industry got off to a bad start in America in 1970. In past years, European designers had always set the standards, and within six months to a year trends that had been applauded in Paris and London were eagerly picked up by fashion-conscious buyers in America.

What *should* have been hot in New York in the fall of 1970 was the calf-length midi, a look Paris designers hoped would replace the miniskirts of the late 1960s. They were so confident, in fact, that one leader of the fashion "establishment" announced, "The whole look of American women will now change, and the die-hard miniskirt adherents are going to be out in the fashion cold."[77]

Backlash Against Designers

But young American women were not impressed with the midi—nor were many men. When major U.S. clothes designers began showing the midi, groups such as GAMS (Girls/Guys Against More Skirt) and FADD (Fight Against Dictating Designers) protested in the streets.

Such a backlash was virtually unheard of, and alarmed American buyers who had invested millions in the midi and the accessories designed for it. "Look, this isn't fun and games," said a fashion coordinator for Manhattan's Bloomingdale's stores. "We have a multi-million dollar business to run, and we're not laughing all the way to the bank. Our whole economy is based on planned obsolescence."[78]

And while some women did purchase midis, the miniskirt remained the hemline of choice, especially among younger buyers. It was an episode in fashion history, say fashion experts, which taught designers a lesson about American women: They would not accept new designs unless

Squash Blossoms and Puka Shells

One of the jewelry fashion fads of the 1970s were puka shell necklaces, which became famous after movie star Elizabeth Taylor wore one in 1974. Puka shells are found in Hawaii, and have a distinctive, doughnut shape. Several shells were strung together and sold for under $6 in Hawaii. After Elizabeth Taylor brought them to the attention of women on the continental United States, however, the price went up to about $150.

An even more expensive jewelry item of the decade was called a "squash blossom"—an American Indian necklace made of hand-tooled silver and turquoise. Squash blossoms were very heavy, at least five or six pounds. The necklace sold for between $300 and $1000.

One could buy a blossom with one large chunk of turquoise, or with six or eight smaller ones arranged in a blossom pattern. The idea was that no two squash blossoms were alike; the color and veining of the turquoise, along with the intricate tooling of the silver, were like individual fingerprints.

According to *Follies and Foibles: A View of 20th Century Fads* by Andrew Marum and Frank Parise, the appeal of Hawaiian and Native American jewelry was its distinctiveness. When you wore it, they write, "you shone alone—you were not just another member of the tribe, trying to be a little exotic and distance yourself from mainstream America."

they liked them. They were no longer willing to abandon a look just because designers mandated they should.

Hot Pants

This newfound freedom from the dictates of designers surfaced soon after the rejection of the midi. Not yet ready to replace the soaring hemlines of the miniskirt, the biggest fashion fad of the early 1970s was hot pants—those short, tight, and skimpy shorts that "revealed more leg and lower cheek than the shortest mini ever had."[79]

Hot pants were more than a craze among high school girls. They were worn by airline flight attendants, bank tellers, and secretaries. Some contestants in the Miss America pageant in 1972 wore them during the obligatory talent competition.

Celebrities, too, were seen in hot pants. Actresses like Jane Fonda and Ursula Andress wore them, Elizabeth Taylor

Actress Elizabeth Taylor sports the latest fashion trend, hot pants, in 1971.

went on a diet so she could wear them, and Jackie Kennedy Onassis had several, including a pair made of black and red leather. (By 1972, there were even a few adventurous men wearing hot pants, including singers David Bowie, Sammy Davis Jr., and Liberace, who wore a red-white-and-blue pair.)

And hot pants seemed appropriate for so many occasions, from very formal to the most casual. The pricey Georgiou's boutiques, for instance, charged $1000 for a white satin pair as part of a formal wedding ensemble. Bloomingdale's department store in New York charged $15 for a pair of gray jeans slashed three inches below the crotch.

Unlike most fashions, hot pants did not originate from one of the great European designers, coming instead from a small boutique in London or Paris. Even so, with the enthusiastic response hot pants received from the public, established firms were forced to produce them anyway. "We prefer not to make hot pants, but we don't have any choice," said one fashion executive. "We don't control the ladies. They control us now."[80]

One disgusted designer was far more pessimistic about the state of American fashion that the hot pants craze represented. "The fashion industry as we know it is dead," he said glumly. "Women are striving toward liberation, and clothes are no longer status; they're very much anti-status. Today fad *equals* fashion."[81]

Pants: A New Alternative

Although hot pants had fairly wide appeal, not everyone was destined to own them. As one fashion magazine warned, "[Hot pants] should sell only to those fashion enthusiasts under, say, 25, and under 36-inch—we hope—hips. The rest—and that's the most—should regard them with the kind of distaste reserved for the measles."[82]

For those women who either couldn't or wouldn't wear hot pants, there was an alternative: pants. Interestingly, as late as 1972 it was still not accepted for women to wear pants in many social situations, such as dining in a fine restaurant. One fashion designer recalls her own embarrassment at being with a woman wearing a pants outfit in New York:

I remember taking an extraordinarily chic young French woman who represented [a French fashion designer] to lunch at a smart restaurant. She was wearing . . . a buttoned jacket over long, cuffed pants. . . . The maitre d', recognizing me, and a little of my (then) anguish, seated us in a side room off the bar, where the condition of my guest couldn't be observed.[83]

By the mid-1970s, however, pants became very common, very acceptable, in almost any situation. They were usually cut very wide, often looking like a skirt until women moved. Some designers attributed the growing women's movement to the demand for pants; others point to the popularity of the 1977 Woody Allen movie, *Annie Hall.* In the film, Diane Keaton wore comfortable, "mannish" clothing, such as baggy pants, waistcoats, tweed jackets, and even ties.

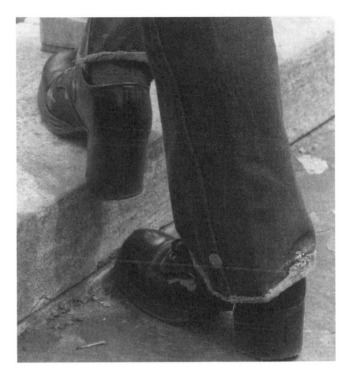

These platform shoes seem modest when compared to today's shoe styles, but some platforms in the 1970s were three inches high.

Platforms and Earth Shoes

Two styles of shoes had their debut, as well as their demise, in the 1970s. The first were called platform shoes, and were considered the most stylish look with hot pants, short skirts, or bell-bottom pants.

Platform shoes were not really any one type of shoe at all, but rather a tall sole, anywhere from one to three inches, added to almost any variety of shoes or boots. Platforms were favorites among glitzy performers such as Elton John, whose sparkling gold and silver boots were decorated with rhinestones and bright polka dots.

They were dangerously high; *Consumer Reports* magazine warned that wearers were in almost constant danger of breaking an ankle. From a design standpoint, many experts argued that the shoes weren't all that attractive. "A moderate platform sole gave height and could look quite elegant," writes one designer, "but the extreme designs were heavily disproportionate to the legs."[84] Another designer agrees, remembering that "it cut the seduction aspect of the [miniskirt] drastically to see a sweet young thing in these clunkers. And, too, the shoes eliminated the wiggle in the walk."[85]

The earth shoe, which was popular at the same time, was reputed to be as healthy as the platform was dangerous. It was designed by Anne Kalso, a Danish yoga instructor, who based the shoe's shape on footprints made by Brazilian Indians in the soft jungle soil. Because they had perfect posture and no known back pain, she decided to replicate the footprints as nearly as possible, with the heel placed lower than the toes.

The "negative heel" shoe was introduced on Earth Day, 1970—hence the name. Millions of pairs of earth shoes were sold in the early- and mid-'70s, although wearers admitted they were not much to look at.

Leisure Suits

Of all men's fashions popular in the 1970s, none was so distinct as the leisure suit. Popular in the early- and mid-1970s, the design was originally introduced following World War II as vacation fashion for wealthy men. Made of wool gabardine, the early leisure suits had a boxy, belted jacket with an inverted pleat. In 1948 one of these suits cost about $100, and came in various bright colors. Men wearing these leisure suits were a common sight on the lush golf courses in Florida and Southern California.

When they were introduced again in the early '70s, leisure suits had a slightly new look. They were made of polyester knit, rather than wool, which made them cheaper than the original. The '70s leisure suit was marketed as "the garment equally at home behind a desk, in a swank restaurant, and at a country club."[86]

They came, writes one observer, "in a jaw-dropping array of Easter-egg pastels, including pink, powder blue, saffron, and tangerine, as well as earth-tone mocha, burnt orange, poison green, crimson, cinnamon, and umber."[87] The top was boxy and often without lapels, cut long and belted. The cuffs had buttons and could be rolled up like shirtsleeves.

The leisure suit failed for a number of reasons. The polyester did not allow one's skin to breathe, so the suits were uncomfortably hot. A second reason—perhaps even more important—is that because they were easy and cheap to manufacture, hundreds of brands of leisure suits flooded every discount store, bargain basement, and sale rack in the country. By the decade's end, a leisure suit in one's closet was an embarrassment. As one observer writes,

"They turned into an emblem of the churl, the bumpkin, and the cheapskate vulgarian."[88]

Jock Chic

The late '60s and early '70s marked the beginning of the American health movement. Words like "cholesterol" were becoming widely used, and people were beginning to pay attention to their weight for more than cosmetic reasons. Health clubs were opening all across the country, and many people bought treadmills and other exercise equipment to use in their homes. More Americans than ever before were becoming vegetarians, and juice bars and health food shops were increasingly common.

This new health consciousness had an effect on fashion, too. Jogging suits, or warm-up suits, became acceptable as suitable attire for more than jogging In June 1972, *Sports Illustrated* declared:

A man and woman model the recent trend, jogging suits. Jogging suits became suitable casual attire both inside and outside the gym.

The hottest thing around may be the warm-up suit. . . . Civilians of all ages, sexes, and shapes are now wearing them everywhere: they turn up on tennis courts and basketball courts, on the golf course and the beach, at the supermarket and in the city streets."[89]

Warm-up suits had a different look than they'd had before, too. No more drab gray sweats, as they had been in decades past. The '70s warm-up suit came in a wide range of colors, and was, as writers Jane and Michael Stern observed, the all-purpose garment:

> Step out of it at night and step into it the next morning; or sleep in it and never take it off. Spill Tang down the front and drip a jelly donut on your lap and let baby spit up on your shoulder. Wear it the next day and the next. Finally, when it becomes too grimy, throw it in the hamper and wear another one.[90]

The warm-up suits of the '70s were different from their predecessors, too, in that they were not designed with utility in mind. Instead of sweat-absorbing cotton, these tightly woven new garments were at least 50 percent polyester, rayon, or some other "miracle fabric" meant to hold their shape and look good.

Wearing such a jogging suit, complete with color-coordinated headband and Nike, Converse, or Adidas sport shoes, made a statement about a person in the '70s. It proclaimed one as being healthy and fit—or at least knowing how to *dress* as though one exercised occasionally.

Pet Rocks

One of the most mindless fads of the 1970s appeared in 1975 and was known as a "pet rock." Pet rocks were the idea of a thirty-eight-year-old advertising man named Gary Dahl, who was tired of the chores and responsiblities of pet ownership. Joking with friends in a bar one evening, he announced a rock as the perfect pet, for it would not need feeding, walking, or grooming.

The idea seemed a little crazy, but he decided to pursue it. Ordering three tons of rocks from a beach in Mexico, Dahl then designed a package (complete with air holes so the pet could breathe) and training manual. To his astonishment, the rocks were an instant fad, becoming *the* hot gift idea for the Christmas of 1975. The rocks sold for $5 each, and 95 cents of that was pure profit for Dahl.

Proud new owners enjoyed reading the training tips for teaching their pets to "play dead" and "roll over" with the help of a gentle nudge from the owner's foot. Like a guard dog, the rock could also protect its owner if he or she were attacked. As Charles Panati explains in *Panati's Parade of Fads, Follies, and Manias,* the manual told the owner to "reach into your pocket and purse as though you were going to comply with the mugger's demands. Extract your pet rock. Shout the command: 'Attack!' and bash the mugger's head in."

Mood Rings

A fad of unbelievable proportions in 1975 was a fashion accessory known as the mood ring, which changed color to fit the wearer's mood. If one was happy, the stone was purple; if one was peaceful, it was blue. A reddish-brown color indicated the wearer was irritable, and if the ring was black, "it meant its wearer was shrouded in gloom, despair, and downright evil karma."[91]

The key to the ring's changeability was a heat-sensitive liquid crystal contained within the stone. The idea belonged to a thirty-three-year-old former Wall Street businessman named Joshua Reynolds, who figured that for about ten cents worth of the liquid crystal, he could transform cheaply made rings into a small fortune. The first day they went on sale in a fashionable New York department store, a thousand sold at $45 each. By December 1975, more than fifteen million had been sold, ranging in price from $250 fourteen-karat-gold rings to cheap rip-offs costing only two or three dollars.

Celebrities like Sophia Loren, Barbra Streisand, and Paul Newman were enthusiastic owners of mood rings, and boxing champion Muhammad Ali even wrote a poem about his ring's uncanny ability. Although it was fun for people to believe that the rings actually reflected their own inner moods, the truth was that only the temperature made the rings change color. One could put a ring on top of a toaster, or even hold it very tight to turn it a vivid blue. Some wanted to advertise a despondent mood and slipped theirs into the refrigerator for a few minutes to turn it black.

Like all fads, the interest in mood rings faded by spring of 1976. The market had become flooded with useless plastic look-alikes, as well as other items such as color-changing watches, shoes, and even underwear.

Back to Basics

One popular fashion of the 1970s which has *not* lost its appeal is blue jeans. They were certainly not new in the '70s. Jeans were invented in the mid-1800s by a tailor named Levi Strauss. Denim jeans were popular in the '30s, '40s, and '50s, especially among teenagers. In the '60s, a tattered, torn pair of jeans became almost a symbol of one's antiestablishment leanings.

In the 1970s, it seemed that almost everyone under forty had at least one pair. One fashion expert wrote that blue denim jeans in the '70s were "the most universally worn garments . . . and the nearest men, women, and children have got to wearing a uniform."[92] The look of

The Rise of the T-Shirt

Never seen in America before World War I, the T-shirt was first noticed by American soldiers in Europe. (They were preferable to the sleeveless, ribbed undershirts of the day because they were softer and more absorbent.) The U.S. Navy issued them as work clothing during World War II, and they became associated with working men. They were almost always white. Almost never did a T-shirt bear any writing or art.

That changed in the 1970s, when according to Jane and Michael Stern in *The Encyclopedia of Bad Taste,* "pop art (which hybridized advertising and personal expression) and activism came together and eradicated ideals of modesty and dignity in clothing." In the 1970s, it became fashionable to wear brightly colored T-shirts with messages emblazoned on the front or back. Shirts proclaimed views on the war in Vietnam, or a favorite rock band. Some shirts were tie-dyed, or were painted with interesting designs. Artist Andy Warhol had a favorite black T-shirt with a picture of a pink and white Good and Plenty box on it.

In 1975 the Anheuser-Busch Brewery saw how T-shirts could be used as advertising when they gave away shirts with the Budweiser beer logo to college students on spring break in Miami and San Diego. The ploy was wildly successful, as the Sterns explain: "To return to school with a Bud shirt became a supreme status symbol among party animals. It became apparent that there was no need to give the shirts away: People would gladly pay to advertise not only Budweiser but Coors and Colt 45 and just about any other favorite product."

early 1970s blue jeans was known as "creative denim." It became very fashionable to decorate jeans with rhinestones, leather fringe, or embroidered flowers. By 1972, patches were added—anything from peace signs, slogans such as "Have a Nice Day," happy faces, and the Rolling Stones' mouth-and-tongue logo.

By the mid-1970s, denim began being used on a wide variety of other products and accessories, too. The After-Six menswear company introduced denim evening jackets with velvet collars. One could buy a denim-covered edition of the Bible and a denim umbrella. Zenith even came out with a "Blue Jean TV," complete with copper rivets.

A Bare Statement

Another fad of the '70s had less to do with clothing than with a lack thereof. It was known as streaking—a short sprint through a public place wearing nothing at all—and it was a very popular phenomenon in 1974.

Although no one knows who was the first streaker, or

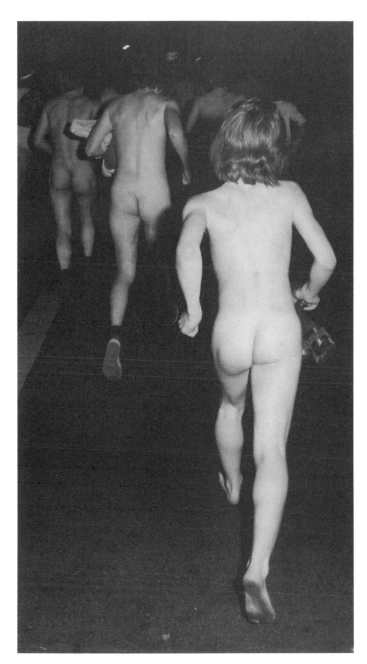

An estimated fifty-five Columbia University streakers run from their campus dormitory and head for the streets of New York.

why it seemed like a good idea, it almost certainly began on a college campus, probably one in a warm climate like Florida or California. It was not meant as a protest or any type of political statement; it was, according to one cultural history, "the Seventies' equivalent of the panty raid of the 1950s."[93]

Streaking was meant to shock and amuse, and the more dignified the public occasion, the more fun it seemed to be. A group of Harvard streakers, wearing only surgical masks, ran though a classroom where students were taking a final exam in anatomy. Streakers dashed through a Rudolf Nureyev ballet solo and disrupted the taping of the *Tonight Show*. There were many reports of streaking that spring at college graduation ceremonies all over the United States.

The most famous incident took place at the Academy Awards, when someone streaked past actor David Niven as he was introducing Elizabeth Taylor. "I

The Itty-Bitty String Thing

The big fashion sensation of the summer of 1974 was the string bikini, which covered nothing in the rear, and next to nothing in the front. In this excerpt from their book Follies and Foibles: A View of 20th Century Fads, *Andrew Marum and Frank Parise explain the beginnings of this hot item, which, they explain, "was to the typical female bathing suit what hot pants were to slacks."*

"What manner of thing was this garment called the string bikini? It was a bikini shaped by two triangles held by cords. One triangle could be seen high up on a woman's body, covering the upper erogenous zones, while the other was lower down, covering the lower erogenous zones. The rest of the body was bare.

In early 1974 string bikinis were first worn by women on Ipanema Beach in Rio de Janeiro. They were so suggestive that the Brazilian military government tried to suppress the wearing of them. The work of no great fashion designer, the string bikini was said to have been patterned after the loincloth that coastal Indians of Brazil used to wear in bygone days. It came in all kinds of fabrics, like chiffon, matte, and cotton.

From Rio de Janeiro the string bikini—or the tanga, as it was known in Brazil, after the ancient Indian word for loincloth—spread to Rome. And from Rome the string bikini came to America, where, by the spring of 1974, it was *the* purchase to make. A string bikini cost between $35 and $45; in Rio the same tanga went for $6 to $10. No matter; they sold out in Bloomingdale's in New York City in two weeks."

suppose it was bound to happen," Niven responded in his clipped British accent, as the audience gasped and tittered. "The only laugh that man will ever get in life is stripping off his pants and showing his shortcomings."[94] By the summer of 1974, the fad was passé.

The Return of Designers

The early '70s saw many Americans, especially women, losing interest in the dictates of the European designers. However, in the late 1970s, there was a return to the status symbol of owning a designer garment. Ironically, the garment was blue jeans!

Although blue jeans had gained in popularity in the '70s, they had not achieved what designers call "chic" status the reputation of being elegantly fashionable. That changed in 1977, however, when two New York garment makers came out with a new line of blue jeans. They used the name Jordache, because it sounded French and classy. With a distinctive symbol on the right rear pocket, the jeans sold well.

By 1979 more than thirty other "designer" jeans had appeared on the market, and the patches, rhinestones, and fringe of the early '70s was passé. With names like Gloria Vanderbilt, Calvin Klein, Sassoon, jeans had become chic—and expensive. In 1979, Calvin Klein had the most costly jeans on the market, at $55 a pair. Even so, they were selling at the rate of a quarter of a million pairs a week. Consumers had strayed a long way from their disinterest in designers at the decade's beginning!

Chapter Six

The Jackson 5, shown here performing on their own television special in 1971, were a pop music sensation during the early years of the decade.

Music of the Seventies

Evolving from a combination of rhythm and blues, country, and pop music, rock and roll was born in the 1950s. In that decade, Elvis Presley was certainly the dominant musical figure. In the 1960s, there was an invasion of British bands, most importantly the Beatles, who were, according to one music historian, not merely performers, but "the musical and spiritual leaders of a generation."[95]

But by the late 1960s, that group was rocked by quarreling and dissension. And when Paul McCartney filed a legal motion against his fellow Beatles in December 1970 (the first step in officially dissolving their partnership), their disbanding became final, which ended the existence of the most popular rock band in the history of music.

So important were the Beatles, in fact, that many experts believe the 1970s were marked more by their demise than by any other musical group's presence. "Having dominated the 60s with their talent," one commentator observes, "the Beatles haunted much of the 70s with their absence, as every fan and critic looked for the next Fab Four."[96]

Growing Audience, Changing Sound

The rock and roll audience looking for "the next big thing" in the 1970s was far different than in decades past. By the 1970s, the number of fans had ballooned. No longer were rock fans merely teenagers; the music was listened to and the records were bought by a much larger segment of the population. The fans who had once shrieked and screamed when the Beatles first performed were solidly in their twenties; those who had gone wild for Elvis and others of the 1950s were in their thirties. "In the previous decade," writes one expert, "rock was the stuff of the counterculture; in the 1970s . . . this music was the culture."[97]

And while the adults of the '50s and '60s had rolled their eyes at the loud music their children listened to,

by the 1970s, says one music historian, the staying power of rock music was no longer a question:

For the first time in its history, large numbers of people began to think that maybe rock and roll really was here to stay; that it could grow and become an artistic medium that could adapt to its aging audience as well as continue to attract young fans who would remain the lifeblood of the music.[98]

Not only had the audience changed, the music itself had undergone a transformation since its birth. For one thing, the music known as "rock and roll" (which in the '70s became known simply as "rock") had become very diversified. Thanks in large measure to the Beatles' experimentation with different types of music, rock no longer needed a predictable beat and chording, as it had through the '50s and most of the '60s.

Some rock music was heavy and strident, some was light and melodic. Some was jazzy, while some used string quartets and had a classical feel—but it was all rock. Indeed, says one music historian, "the Beatles had shown that virtually anything, from Indian raga to your last acid flashback, could inspire the composition of a rock song."[99]

It would have been almost impossible for another musician or musical

Society's Diversity and the Music Industry

In this excerpt from Rock & Roll: Its History and Stylistic Development, *Joe Stuessy explains how the complexity and fragmentation of society as a whole led to a completely varied menu of music in the 1970s.*

"Society fragmented into hundreds of subcategories of self-interest groups. The relative simplicity of the old demographics—male and female, youth and adult, black and white, lower, middle, and upper class—fragmented into a complex array of demographic clusters. The sellers of products and services responded accordingly. A specially designed product or service was made available for each minicategory within the society. As John Naisbitt wrote in *Megatrends,* we moved from an 'either/or' society to a 'multiple option' society.

Naisbitt points out that [in the '70s] the automobile industry offered 752 different models, including 126 different 'subcompacts'; there were over 200 brands of cigarettes; a store in Manhattan specialized in light bulbs, offering 2,500 different types. By the end of the decade, instead of three television networks, cable systems offered the viewer over forty choices. Grocers offered not just mustard but everything from peanut mustard to all-natural, salt-free Arizona champagne mustard. There were magazines for every conceivable minigroup; the book stores were stuffed with self-help books on everything from diets to how to make a million dollars.

The music industry was no different. Radio discovered the concept of 'formatting,' that is, programming certain styles of music for a very specific audience who typically purchased a predictable set of advertised products. [Here are] a partial list of such formats: album-oriented rock, easy-listening pop, big-band jazz, progressive jazz, disco, punk rock, rhythm and blues, oldies but goodies, country rock, rock country, progressive rock. To this list could be added Top 40, classical music, ethnic music, Christian programming, talk radio, and all news. . . .

The world waited for the next Presley or Beatles but slowly began to realize that that was no longer possible. The music market (indeed, society as a whole) was so fragmented that no one person or group could possibly cut across all those radio formats, all those record bins, and all those demographic minigroups. For a while each new artist was hailed as the new giant—for example, Elton John, Peter Frampton, and the Bee Gees. But in such a fragmented market there simply could not be such a figure."

group to appeal to such a wide range of musical tastes that had been created by the late 1960s, and to be as well received as the Beatles had been. Even so, there were plenty who tried.

"Glam Rock"

One style of rock that was very popular in the early 1970s was known as "glitter rock" or "glam rock," which brought flashy new techniques, such as expensive laser lighting and electronic synthesizers to concerts. Glam rockers wore heavy makeup and outrageous costumes, and the emphasis was less on the music itself than on the theatrics of the performance. Beatle John Lennon once termed it "just rock and roll with lipstick on,"[100] but its fans found it much more than that.

The look of a glam rocker was far different from the longhaired singers of the '60s. In fact, long hair was no longer the shocking mark of rebellion, as it had been a decade before. By the time 1970 arrived, in fact, so many boys wore their hair shoulder-length or longer, that it no longer made a statement. The gimmick of glam rock was a sort of sexless, glittery look, the most popular glam rocker of all being David Bowie.

No one achieved anywhere near the fame with glam rock as Bowie, a British advertising artist and actor, whom the New York *Daily News* once called "the Elvis of the 70s."[101] His

Popular rock star David Bowie shows off his glam rock fashion while portraying Ziggy Stardust, a character who sported orange hair and glittery clothing.

songs were the least important aspect of his concerts. His genius, say music critics, was in his ability to invent "characters" to portray onstage. One of his most famous was Ziggy Stardust, who one writer called "a grotesque and beautiful, bisexual rock-and-roll alien, with white powder makeup, flaming orange woodpecker hair, stacked boots, and glitter."[102]

While many glam rock acts were intent only on shocking their audiences—such as Kiss's use of fake blood-vomit, onstage explosions and fires, and rocket-firing guitars—Bowie drew mostly praise from music critics for his sensitive lyrics and high drama.

The Mellow Sound

As far from the glitter and makeup of glam rock as could be was the mellow, personal sound of singer-songwriters like James Taylor, Carole King, Joni Mitchell, Jim Croce, and Neil Young. These artists tended to use fairly simple instrumentation—piano or acoustic guitar—rather than the heavy electric sounds of other rockers of the day.

The singer-songwriters of the '70s were not an entirely new sound; others such as Arlo Guthrie, Bob Dylan, and Simon and Garfunkel had had great success with their guitar-strumming styles. The key difference, however, was the focus of the songs. While the folk singers of years past had sung about the evils of war, racism, and the struggles of the working people, these new singer-songwriters were more intimate. Their music often looked inward, and they sang about their own ambitions, friendships, and relationships.

Singer-songwriter James Taylor was such a musician in 1970, according to expert Ken Tucker, conveying "almost no sense that there was a big world out there, that there were social issues and problems bigger than his own private obsessions."[103] Taylor, called "the first superstar of the 1970s" in a *Time* cover story in March 1971, came from an affluent North Carolina family. He was plagued by heroin addiction and depression, and was a patient in a mental institution for a time. Many of his songs, such as "Carolina in My Mind," "Sweet Baby James," and "Fire and Rain," addressed those times in his life. And if there was any greater message in his music, he said in an interview, "I guess it's to look deeply into your own self for answers."[104]

Carole King was another immensely popular singer-songwriter of the decade. She had written several classics in the early '60s, including "The Locomotion," "Go Away, Little Girl," and "Will You Still Love Me Tomorrow," but returned to the music scene in 1971 as a performer as well, with what one critic called a "warm, appealingly worn alto voice."[105]

Her album *Tapestry* sold fifteen million copies, staying at number one for a full fifteen weeks. It was, in 1971, the biggest-selling pop album in history up until that time. Singles such as "It's Too Late," and "I Feel the Earth Move" were popular hits, which remain as strong today as they were in 1971.

The Birth of Heavy Metal

Another variety of rock came into existence in the early 1970s. Its roots were in the rock sound of bands like the Rolling Stones and Cream (Eric Clapton's band), but it was a much harder, more strident sound. Heavy metal, as this music was called, began as merely an exaggeration of hard rock, as one expert explains:

> If hard rock was loud, heavy metal was louder; if hard rock was simple and repetitive, heavy metal was simpler and more repetitive; if hard rock singers shouted, heavy metal singers screamed; if hard rockers experimented with electronic distortion and feedback, heavy metalers

distorted everything; if hard rock was *countercultural*, heavy metal would come to specialize in the *anticultural.*[106]

The British group Led Zeppelin was the most influential of all the heavy metal bands. Their "Stairway to Heaven" and "Whole Lotta Love"

The generation gap really widened with heavy metal rock bands like Led Zeppelin. Parents hated what they called noisy, tuneless music, while teenagers rocked out to the mantralike high speed guitar playing.

Led Zeppelin Trivia

In their book The Seventies: From Hot Pants to Hot Tubs, *Andrew J. Edelstein and Kevin McDonough have compiled a list of interesting "factoids" about Led Zeppelin. The following is an excerpt from that list.*

- The bands first choices for a name were the Mad Dogs and Whoopie Cushion. Instead, they recalled a suggestion by Who drummer Keith Moon. He had often used the expression "going down like a lead zeppelin" to describe horrendous gigs. Page [one of the group's leaders] suggested changing "lead" to "led" so that Americans wouldn't pronounce the name as "leed."
- They played a 1970 concert in Copenhagen under the name the Nobs, because a German woman named Eva von Zeppelin objected to the band's use of her family's name.

- The group reached its absolute height of popularity in March 1975. Powered by the release of *Physical Graffiti*, all six Zeppelin LPs placed on the Billboard charts. In January three Madison Square Garden concerts sold out in only four hours.
- The group was mentioned positively by the two U.S. presidential candidates in the 1976 election. Gerald Ford's daughter Susan stated on *The Dick Cavett Show* that Zeppelin was her favorite band. Jimmy Carter, while addressing the National Association of Record Manufacturers, recalled listening to Zeppelin music during all-night sessions at the Georgia governor's mansion.
- Two of their most popular LPs, *Led Zeppelin IV* . . . and *Houses of the Holy*, had neither the title nor the group's name printed on their album jackets. Both went to the top three.

earned them number one spots on the charts throughout the United States in the early '70s, even though the band at first was dismissed by many adults as "little more than a pile of noise." [107] Expert Timothy White describes the sound of their first album, unlike anything he had ever heard before:

> Its hollow, thudding percussion, stupored melodies and strangled, clarion vocals suggested a somnambulistic Goliath in the throes of an opium trance. The playing

was blues-based but coated with fuzzy overtones and splenetic distortion. This was "heavy metal," fully realized in all its precise, ponderous pomp. [108]

With the screeching feedback and distortion of guitarist Jimmy Page and the screaming vocals of Robert Plant, Led Zepplin actually beat out the Beatles as "most popular group" in a British teen opinion poll late in 1970 (although, to be fair, the Beatles had split up by then).

How Bad Can Rock Get?

As abrasive as heavy metal was, and as distasteful as that music was to many parents of teens in the mid-1970s, there was another fragment of the rock scene that was even more harsh and strident. It was known as punk rock, and it remains one of the most lasting images of rebellious youth and rock music of that decade.

Punk rock got its start in New York, when bands such as the Ramones and the New York Dolls gained popularity. The bands and their fans wore ripped clothing, often adorned with studs and safety pins, and sang songs like "Now I Wanna Sniff Some Glue," "Blitzkrieg Bop," and "I Want to Be Sedated." They often shaved their heads, put safety pins through their noses, and wore Mohawks dyed vivid green, pink, or orange.

The punk movement was the ultimate rebellion—not just against mainstream society, or the older generation—but against their fellow rock musicians, whom they accused of blatant commercialism and "selling out" by creating music that was pure sentimentalism. Punk was, writes one expert, "a reaction to the increasing pride in technical virtuosity that was overrunning rock on every level, from the elaborate instruments used to create the music to the scientifically researched ways a major rock tour was mounted and executed." [109]

The result was simpler, louder, shorter songs, with more gross and obscene lyrics than had been used before. There were neither attempts at fancy instrumentation nor long solos by punk performers. When they did concerts, their onstage antics were offensive—whether electrocuting small animals, beheading dolls with a guillotine, or slapping members of the audience, who didn't seem to mind at all. With punk rock, music was not the most important thing, as Rolling Stones bandmember Keith Richard noted, "It was more important if you puked over somebody." [110]

The Sex Pistols

Punk might have stayed a New York phenomenon, except for the rise in popularity of a British punk band called the Sex Pistols. They were crude and offensive, and this contributed to their popularity. For instance, their first performance was at St. Martin's College in London, on November 6, 1975, and it was widely reported that the school secretary was so incensed at the crudity that he cut off the band's electrical supply after just a few songs.

The leader of the Sex Pistols was a young man named, aptly enough,

Members of the rock band the Sex Pistols—with Johnny Rotten at center, perform for the camera. The group, one of the most notorious punk-rock bands, was famous for its crudity and vulgarity.

Johnny Rotten. Rotten was rude and offensive not only on stage, but during interviews, as well. After one appearance on a British television show, Rotten swore vulgarly at the host, prompting thousands of outraged telephone calls to the station demanding the group be banned.

One newspaper reported that a forty-seven-year-old truck driver, shocked that his young son had been exposed to such vile language, kicked in his television set. "It blew up and I was knocked backwards," the man said. "I was so angry and disgusted with this filth that I took a swing with my boot. . . . I don't want this sort of muck coming into my home at teatime." [111]

The disgust most parents felt toward Rotten and the rest of the Sex

Priestesses of Punk

In addition to the male groups like the Sex Pistols, the Ramones, and the Velvet Underground that made it big in punk rock—there were also some very successful young women. Many of them were known as much for their definitive dress as their singing voices.

Patti Smith was considered a poet of punk rock, and dressed in up to twelve layers of cardigans, men's shirts, ties, and jackets. Occasionally she used another look—that of a loose-fitting, wrinkled dress with men's unlaced workboots. When asked about her style (or lack of) she claimed she was paying homage to some of her singing heroes—Jim Morrison of the Doors, Bob Dylan, and Jimi Hendrix, to name a few.

Another famous woman punker was Debbie Harry, the lead singer of the group Blondie. She enjoyed shocking her audience, and occasionally dressed in a white lace wedding dress and veil, and then ripped it off while singing her hit "Rip Her to Shreds."

Punk rocker Patti Smith shocked people with her crude rock lyrics and abrasive, raspy voice.

Pistols didn't bother him. He continued to write and sing songs like "God Save the Queen (She Ain't a Human Being)," which was promptly banned by British television and radio stations. The band concentrated more on guest appearances in the United States, and in more live concerts, where they slashed themselves with razor blades and broken bottles.

Although the Sex Pistols and other punk rockers played up the violence and vulgarity of their acts, they commented time and time again that the older generation wasn't properly understanding them. "All we're trying to do," explained Johnny Rotten, shrugging, "is destroy everything."[112]

Disco

No other style of music, however, says "1970s" quite as much as disco, the phenomenon that began in 1974 with the Hues Corporation's hit "Rock the Boat," and George McCrae's "Rock Your Baby." Disco exploded into popularity by 1975, and peaked in 1977–78 with the Bee Gees and the movie *Saturday Night Fever*. On April 2, 1979, disco star Donna Summer was on the cover of *Newsweek*, and the magazine proclaimed that "Disco Is Here to Stay." By 1980, disco was all but dead. What happened?

Although there is no question that disco was a '70s phenomenon, the beginnings of disco lay in the late '60s, when various countercultural groups (gay, black, Latino) combined as an alternative to the white male–dominated rock scene. The music was a mixture of different styles, says one expert:

[It was] the latest incarnation of rhythm and blues (or rhythm without the blues, as *Newsweek* noted), foremost among them James Brown's make-it-funky beat and [soul singer Kenny] Gamble and [Leon] Huff's sweet and soulful Philadelphia International sound; the icy synthesizer-dominated sound known as Eurodisco, with a hint of the melodies of jazz and swing."[113]

The beat of disco, too, was distinct—quick-paced and throbbing, usually 125 beats per minute.

Early in 1974 several disco hits were released, and the music became more mainstream, more inclusive. Here was music that begged to be danced to, and people did, dressed in their '70s best, with platform shoes, tight pants, spandex, and glittery halter tops. It was, remember authors Andrew Edelstein and Kevin McDonough, proof that the '60s style of music was over and done:

You had to get dressed up to go out. You actually had to learn

John Travolta and Karen Gorney head for the dance floor in the film Saturday Night Fever. *The soundtrack from the album sold over twenty-five million copies to become the best-selling soundtrack of all time.*

dance steps. You probably had to cut your hair to fit in. Spending money on material goods and designer merchandise became desirable ends. Unlike rock music, you weren't expected to experience the music in your head: it was a pure bodily sensation. It was totally apolitical; its only message was to dance, party, and have fun.[114]

Disco clubs, with disc jockeys cleverly using two turntables to pro-

vide "seamless" dancing as well as pulsing colored lights, were *the* place to go on a Friday or Saturday night.

Disco Sucks

Disco became even more of a rage with the 1977 release of *Saturday Night Fever,* starring John Travolta as a young working-class New Yorker who strives to become a disco champion. The recording, highlighted by such hits as "Stayin' Alive" and "How Deep Is Your

Love?" became the biggest-selling soundtrack of all time, with over twenty-five million albums sold. Disco might have seemed to some observers to be firmly entrenched in the fabric of society, but it was not to be.

By 1979, having become so commercial, disco had become something of a joke. Radio stations were having antidisco crusades. Graffiti proclaiming "Death to Disco" was seen in public bathrooms as punk and heavy metal fans lashed out against the disco style. And on "Disco Sucks" night at Chicago's Comiskey Park on July 12, 1979, hundreds of disco albums were set into crates and burned as the crowd roared its approval.

But although the disco craze was widespread for a time, it was certainly *not* the essence of '70s music; therefore its well-publicized "death" was not the end of all music of the decade. Quite the contrary: the varied forms of popular music that blossomed in the 1970s proved beyond a doubt that rock and roll did not depend on one musical group to thrive. Listeners could look forward to new ways in which the music could reinvent itself in the '80s and beyond.

Chapter Seven

The stars of the blockbuster hit Star Wars—*Mark Hamill, Carrie Fisher, and Harrison Ford. Directed by George Lucas, the film was a megahit, earning $256 million in ticket sales alone.*

Television and Film in the Seventies

Both television and film changed a great deal in the 1970s, in terms of the style of production and in the content. There were innovations and landmarks in both media. But it was television, by far, that reinvented itself during the decade.

For many Americans it may be difficult to imagine television in the 1970s, before VCRs were found in most homes, before "cable" offered more choices than merely the three large networks. The '70s was a crucial decade for television, one during which great strides were made not only in the range of the types of programs, but in the content, as well.

Some historians have noted that television in the 1970s surely mirrored American society's concerns.

The first part of the decade reflected the lingering social and political concerns of the '60s; by the middle and late '70s, people were more interested in escapism and nostalgia.

"Not Much to Satisfy the Youth of America"

One might think that in 1970, American television would reflect society. Unrest on college campuses and the antiwar sentiment that had been a mark of the late 1960s continued to be a hallmark of a growing youth movement. However, looking over a copy of *TV Guide* from that year would indicate nothing of the sort.

What shows *were* in prime time were Westerns, such as *Gunsmoke, The High Chaparral,* and *Bonanza.* There were sitcoms, like *Mayberry R.F.D., That Girl,* and *My Three Sons.* And variety shows—Doris Day, Glen Campbell, Tim Conway, Carol Burnett, Dean Martin, Johnny Cash, Andy Williams—the list goes on and on.

There was certainly not a great deal for teens and young adults. Television executives had made some effort in the late '60s to make TV relevant to young people by developing shows such as *The Mod Squad* and *The Rookies* (both police shows with blacks as main characters), but for the most part, the offerings by the three major networks had very little to do with how young people were feeling at the time. As social historians Edelstein and McDonough recall:

> On May 4, 1970, as four students were being killed by Ohio National Guardsmen at Kent State, TV viewers could have seen: Doris Day fouling up a computer company's electric bill on *The Doris Day Show*, the gang from *Mayberry R.F.D.* visiting Palm Springs, and Lucille Ball masquerading as a gum-chewing blond secretary on *Here's Lucy.* Not much to satisfy the youth of America there.[115]

Putting the Sixties on TV

Things changed abruptly on Tuesday, January 12, 1971. That was when an announcer's voice came on after *Hee Haw* and warned viewers that the program to follow would "throw a humorous spotlight on our frailties, prejudices, and concerns. By making them a source of laughter, we hope to show—in a mature fashion—just how absurd they are."[116]

The show was a half-hour situation comedy called *All in the Family*, about a loading dock foreman named Archie Bunker who had prejudices toward everyone. He was sexist, racist, and homophobic. He hated protesters, whom he called "pinkos." He freely used words like "fag," "spic," and "spade" —heretofore considered totally inappropriate on television.

As one television expert notes, the language Archie Bunker used was certainly nothing new, and neither were his narrow-minded ideas.

They'd been in the papers, on the news, and in private conversation for decades. Their emergence in prime time denoted not their newness, but rather, the recognition that after a while, hiding one's head in the sand just adds up to a sandy head. The ideas themselves were not about to go away, but it took the Seventies to put the Sixties on TV.[117]

Getting "All Wet at Once"

All in the Family was the creation of Norman Lear, who understood how nervous the network executives were about the content of the show. In fact, CBS had suggested to Lear that he ease the audience into the show by airing a

The cast of the popular hit TV sitcom All in the Family: *(from bottom to top) Carroll O'Connor, Jean Stapleton, Rob Reiner, and Sally Struthers. The show broke new ground in many areas, including openly discussing such sensitive issues as racism, bigotry, and family problems.*

few nonthreatening episodes first. But Lear refused, insisting that the only way to enter into such new, unchartered territory was to dive right in and "get all wet at once."[118] CBS reluctantly

Archie Meets His Maker

One of the topics often addressed in All in the Family *was religion. Archie had a running argument with just about everyone as to the nature of God—his feminist neighbor Irene, his nonbelieving son-in-law Mike, and his black neighbors, the Jeffersons. In this excerpt from their book* Favorite Families on TV, *authors Christopher and Michael Denis relate how Archie's views changed—at least for the moment.*

"Archie is bugged at his Italian neighbor, Irene Lorenzo (played by Betty Garrett). She is a *female* who knows how to fix things better than he does and puts a new safety lock and automatic closer on his basement door. He is waiting for the oil men to come and service his heater.

After Irene leaves, and the house is deserted, he goes into the basement to check the heater and accidently locks himself in. The house is cold, and his family won't be home for hours. Archie finds some liquor—'his blanket in a bottle'—and gets smashed trying to keep warm. 'I could croak down here, and nobody would know,' [he mourns].

Reeling drunkenly, he decides to make out a will. To Mike [his son-in-law], he leaves his American flag (with forty-eight stars). To [daughter] Gloria, 'who I forgive for marrying above-mentioned, my personal living room chair' to be the centerpiece of her new home. 'To Mrs. Irene Lorenzo, who killed me,' he gives a wet raspberry. Edith [his wife] he feels will be provided for, because 'God takes care of dingbats.'

Archie harangues a contrite and nervous Edith in a typical scene from All in the Family.

Impatient to meet his maker, Archie calls on God to 'take me out of this joint.' To his amazement he hears a knock. 'Is that you down there, Mr. Bunker?' 'Yeah, Lord.' 'Hold on, I'm coming for you.' Footsteps on the stairs. A black man, the *oil man*, with a beard and a mellifluous voice, steps out of the shadows. Mouth agape, Archie falls to his knees, crying, 'Forgive me, Lord. The Jeffersons was right!'"

agreed, but hired fifty additional switchboard operators, for they were sure that the lines would be jammed with angry viewers.

There were calls, but far fewer negative ones than predicted. The show won two Emmy awards the following May, Outstanding Comedy Series and Best Actress in a Comedy Series to Jean Stapleton, who played Archie's wife, Edith. And by the following fall, the show was the number one rated show in America.

Many felt the show's success was Archie's ability to be three-dimensional —more than just a bigot. Lear admitted that could be true; he had modeled Archie after his father, he said, who had the same kinds of prejudices. "I could never forgive him for being a bigot," says Lear, "but I found that there were other things to love him for."[119] Evidently, the viewers of America could do the same for Archie Bunker, for many of the show's biggest fans turned out to be those who were the butt of Archie's name-calling tirades.

There was no doubt that *All in the Family* broke new ground in television programming. Not only were certain words used that had never been on television before, but Archie and the other characters addressed issues that were considered too sensitive for viewers. During its twelve-year run between 1971 and 1983, topics such as homosexuality, rape, vasectomies, miscarriages, and interracial marriage were all woven into the show.

"It Has Become Fashionable to . . . Go Home at 9 on Saturday"

The Mary Tyler Moore Show was another groundbreaker, but in a much softer, gentler way. The program, which ran from the fall of 1970 until 1977, was created for Mary Tyler Moore, who had played Dick Van Dyke's wife, Laura, in the very successful *Dick Van Dyke Show* of the 1960s. Network executives were nervous, however, because of the way writers were creating her character, Mary Richards.

As originally scripted, Mary was a divorcée—something that had never been done in a sitcom before. Executives were strongly against her being divorced— they worried that people would feel as though she were divorced from Dick Van Dyke, her former television husband. They tried to persuade the writers to make Mary a widow, but that didn't seem to fit. And they were worried about making her just a single woman, because they felt that she might be viewed as a lesbian. Such were the stereotypes of the early '70s.

Finally it was decided that Mary had been engaged, but had been jilted.

Ed Asner and Mary Tyler Moore on the set of the popular Mary Tyler Moore
Show. *Mary's role as a single, capable woman in a job surrounded by not-so-
enlightened men portrayed feminism in a gentle, comic way.*

Regardless, the show was a pioneer in that it broke from the norm—the sit-com that revolved around a family. Explains one expert, "The series focused on the travails of a growing segment of society which television, until then, had ignored—namely single adults, and particularly women."[120] In addition, she was rarely paired up with a man, a fact that exhibited her individuality.

Critics did not know what to make of the show at first, probably because it was so different from anything that had ever aired. After its first episode, *Time* called it "a disaster for the old co-star of 'The Dick Van Dyke Show,'" and the *New York Times* dismissed the show as "a preposterous item."[121] However, like *All in the Family*, it became a hit with the young audience. One critic wrote in 1971 that *The*

Mary Tyler Moore Show "is so In, actually, that it has become especially fashionable to drift into the den at a party—or even go home at 9 on a Saturday because you simply must not miss the program."[122]

From *Good Times* to *Sanford and Son*

There was another change that began in the 1970s—the end of the white monopoly. Since the mid-1950s, there were few nonwhite faces, except for an occasional sidekick, such as Rochester, Jack Benny's comic housekeeper, or Jay Silverheels who played Tonto on *The Lone Ranger*. The only lead in a sitcom played by a non-white was Diahann Carroll, who played in NBC's *Julia*.

But *All in the Family* had opened doors that had not been open before. Archie's neighbor George Jefferson, a black man as bigoted as Archie, proved so popular with viewers that Norman Lear eventually produced *The Jeffersons* as a separate show. Here was a black leading man (played by Sherman Hemsley) who blacks believed talked right, sounded right, and

said things Julia would never have said.

Norman Lear was just as successful with two other shows about black families: *Good Times* and *Sanford and Son*. The first took place on the opposite end of the economic scale from

Demond Wilson as Lamont, LaWanda Page as Aunt Esther, and Redd Foxx as Fred Sanford on the set of television's Sanford and Son. *Several shows that featured black families became popular in the 1970s.*

the Jeffersons'—the low-income Cabrini-Greene housing project in Chicago (the Jeffersons had moved from Archie's neighborhood, to a large apartment in Manhattan). *Sanford and Son* was set in Watts, and starred comedian Redd Foxx as grouchy junk dealer Fred Sanford who was constantly berating his son Lamont (played by Demond Wilson).

Like Archie Bunker and George Jefferson, Fred Sanford was narrow-minded and prejudiced, and this made many critics wonder if television was "glorifying" bigotry by making it funny. Defenders of the shows, however, were adamant that such programs made the subject of racial prejudice a little easier for people to approach. As one '70s historian notes, "Instead of preaching to the audience . . . Lear brought up issues and let the audience draw their own conclusions—which they did."[123]

"Live . . . from New York . . ."

Comedy wasn't found only in sitcoms during the '70s. In 1975 NBC launched *Saturday Night Live*, a ninety-minute program that started after the late news on Saturdays. It was to late-night TV what *All in the Family* and other new sitcoms were to prime-time. It was the network's way to pull in younger viewers who would otherwise

have a choice of reruns of Johnny Carson or an old movie.

Saturday Night Live premiered in rather grim times. In 1975, President Ford's administration was trying to heal the anger and bitterness the nation felt after Watergate, OPEC's oil prices were going through the roof, and the economic outlook for America was grim. Even so, the "Not Ready for Prime Time Players," featuring Chevy Chase, Dan Akroyd, John Belushi, and other newcomers were able to make people laugh.

The show was sarcastic in tone, clearly eager to poke fun of anything "establishment." Chevy Chase did wildly overdone impersonations of Gerald Ford falling and tripping, the Weekend Update was a mockery of the news, and many of the best skits mocked television itself. It was, say cultural historians, a concept whose time had definitely come. "[The show] soon became a kind of cultural lightning rod," writes one, "for all the disillusioned creative energy that had nowhere else to go in the anxious mid-1970s."[124]

Lorne Michaels, who created the show, agrees that *Saturday Night Live* needed that "disillusioned creative energy" to forge comedy that was different from the typical variety show fare (appealing to older viewers) that was on television in the '70s. He explains,

From Skits to Popular Folklore

Saturday Night Live did more than attract viewers on what normally was a slow television time. As it succeeded in drawing a larger and larger audience, say Jane and Michael Stern in their Encyclopedia of Pop Culture, many of the show's characters and bits of the 1970s, '80s, and '90s became part of the ·popular folklore of the time.

The cast of Saturday Night Live *in the 1970s included many stars who would go on to become hugely popular in film and television, including Jane Curtin (far left), Laraine Newman (second from left), Bill Murray and Dan Akroyd (center), Gilda Radner, and John Belushi.*

- John Belushi as the samurai warrior in a mundane job, starting with a "Samurai Hotel" sketch and including "Samurai Tailor" and "Samurai Psychiatrist."
- Gilda Radner as Emily Litella, who does an op-ed segment on "Weekend Update" based on her misunderstanding of a common term (such as "Soviet jewelry" rather than "Soviet Jewry"), then, when her mistake is pointed out, meekly says, "Never mind."
- Chevy· Chase as a hopelessly clumsy President Gerald Ford.
- The Coneheads, from the planet Remulac (Dan Akroyd, Jane Curtin, Laraine Newman) masquerading as earthlings, but never getting it exactly right.
- Bill Murray as Nick, the unctuous lounge singer.
- Steve Martin and Dan Akroyd as Jorge and Yortuk Festrunk, the swinging Czech brothers, famous for their flowered shirts and geeky seduction techniques, which usually involved rhapsodizing about "large American breasts."
- Don Novello as Father Guido Sarducci, chain-smoking gossip columnist for the Vatican newspaper.
- Dan Akroyd and John Belushi as the Blues Brothers (which started as a bit within a "Killer Bee" sketch), then became a preshow warm-up act.

Weekend Update, a regular feature of Saturday Night Live, *features Chevy Chase as anchor, Jane Curtin, and Gilda Radner. The show remains a popular hit today.*

I wanted to get away from that by coming to New York instead of L.A., by going on live, by taking chances, and by keeping it as much like theatre as possible. The feeling of outlaw here is strong—and I think that's what the audiences respond to.[125]

The show definitely succeeded as a ratings hit; like *The Mary Tyler Moore Show*, it gave younger audiences a reason to stay home on Saturday nights. Too, it gave a career boost to a host of

rising young comedians in the late '70s, '80s, and '90s, such as Billy Crystal, Julia Louis-Dreyfus, Dana Carvey, Bill Murray, and Jane Curtin.

The Birth of the Miniseries

Another novelty in the 1970s was the miniseries, a very long movie broken into several evenings of viewing time. The first miniseries were British-made, such as the critically acclaimed *Upstairs, Downstairs,* and were transplanted to American television, where they had enthusiastic, but small, audiences. American networks weren't sure how to make the format popular with viewers in the United States. Wouldn't people find it annoying to have to tune in again and again to follow one movie? Wouldn't they find it troublesome if they missed the first segment to catch up in the second or third?

The Public Broadcasting Network's *Masterpiece Theatre* tried the first American miniseries by showing *Rich Man, Poor Man,* a twelve-hour movie, over the span of several weeks in 1976. But the idea of an American miniseries really took off with the made-for-television adaptation of Alex Haley's book *Roots.*

Roots was the story of black author Haley's search for his own roots, beginning with the kidnapping of a young African, Kunta Kinte, who was brought to America as a slave, and would become Haley's great-great-great-great grandfather. The show proceeded through several generations of slavery and abuse at the hands of white Americans, and ends with freedom after the Civil War.

"It Doesn't Sound Like a Good Idea"

The idea sounded interesting to producer David Wolper, and he took the idea to ABC. He had to convince network executives that it would work, however, for they thought that a predominantly white audience might be reluctant to watch a twelve-hour show about blacks. As one high-ranking network executive said, "Here's twelve

A scene from the popular miniseries Roots. *Although at first reluctant to produce a twelve-hour show about black history, ABC was pleasantly surprised when the miniseries captured 85 percent of the viewing public.*

hours of a story where the whites are the villains and the blacks are the heroes in a country that is 85 percent white. It doesn't sound like a good idea at first blush."[126]

ABC finally agreed to try it, and committed more than $6 million to the project. The cast was considered blue-chip at the time, and included Ed Asner, Ben Vereen, LeVar Burton, Cicely Tyson, and O.J. Simpson. It aired over eight consecutive nights, instead of once a week, as *Rich Man, Poor Man* had been shown.

The doubts of the network disappeared after the airing of the first segment on January 23, 1977. It won the highest ratings that night, and for each of the next nights it aired. An estimated 85 percent of the households with television sets watched all or part of it. It became, according to one cultural history of the '70s, a national event:

> People canceled meetings, movie attendance declined, and even members of Congress asked for early adjournment so they could rush home and watch that evening's installment. In some bars, patrons actually switched off basketball games and put on *Roots* instead.[127]

And those who had worried about the disinterest of white Americans were proven wrong. William Greider of the *Washington Post* called *Roots* "a stunning passage in the mass culture of America. . . . [It] allows white Americans to watch that terrible racial history and instead of consuming guilt, they are encouraged to say to themselves— hey—that's my story, too."[128]

Return to Nostalgia

By the mid-1970s, there was a new trend in television: nostalgia. Historians say that because of the recession, Watergate and the distrust of government, the fall of Vietnam, and the energy crisis, people had had enough of reality to last them for a while. While "relevant" television programs like *All in the Family* and others based on real life remained popular, there was a growing need for people to escape.

There was a variety of nostalgia from which viewers could choose. Michael Landon starred in a series called *Little House on the Prairie*, which told the story of a pioneer family in Minnesota. *The Waltons* starred Richard Thomas in a nostalgic look at the depression through the eyes of a rural Virginia teenager.

The most popular of the nostalgia shows was ABC's *Happy Days,* a look back at the '50s. Like other shows of this ilk, *Happy Days* tended to gloss over the more unpleasant aspect of the times, focusing instead on the simplicity and easier pace of life. The most intriguing character on the show was a leather-jacketed renegade named Arthur Fonzarelli, or "The Fonz," as everyone called him. His trademark "thumbs up" and "Ayyyy!" were copied by grade school boys and girls throughout America.

The Movies of Blaxploitation

Just as the television industry went through major changes in the '70s, the motion picture industry was evolving, too. One of the best examples of this was the industry's new attention to young black audiences. At the beginning of the decade, black actors who landed parts in movies were most often cast as either villains, slaves, or soft-spoken, nonpolitical characters that seemed to most blacks very different from themselves. Says one film historian, "Black popular audiences were starving for black heroes who were not made for white audiences." [129]

The early 1970s saw a host of movies known as "blaxploitation" films, because of their rush to cash in on young black audiences. Among these films were *Sweet Sweetback's Baadasssss Song, Superfly, Black Caesar, Trouble Man,* and perhaps the most widely seen, *Shaft.* The movies were similar in that the heroes were streetwise and tough private eyes or secret

agents. The studio that released *Shaft* described John Shaft, the central character in the movie, as "a lone, black Superspade—a man of flair and flamboyance who has fun at the expense of the (white) establishment." [130] And as the lyrics to *Shaft's* theme song indicated ("Who's the black private dick who's a sex machine to all the chicks?") the heroes are sexually active—a trait earlier white-made films about blacks did not address.

The making of blaxploitation movies did not arise from a desire in Hollywood to promote racial harmony; the motivation was pure money. As one black producer noted at the time, "White filmmakers aren't really seeing black. They're seeing black and green." [131] The movies *were* successful. For example, *Sweetback* was made for less than $500,000, and made more than $4 million in theaters.

However, even though the films were moneymakers, they received a great deal of criticism. Many women's groups protested that black filmmakers were stereotyping black women, something that had always been done to black men. Some critics complained that these films tended to be very predictable, in that the black hero would always win out over racist white villains. Wrote one *New York Times* critic,

It may be personally ego-gratifying for blacks to see one of their own stick it to the Man, but what these films have failed to do is go beyond their limited medium of expression and provide something new, something more imaginative than enticement purely on a black vs. white society.[132]

And there was criticism from the black community as well. Many black leaders felt that even though the films showed black men as heroes, they were of questionable heroic stature. They felt that they were as stereotypical as earlier white-made films had been, only in a different way. The settings for such films were all in crime-ridden, inner-city neighborhoods inhabited by the ever-present pimps, pushers, and whores.

The National Association for the Advancement of Colored People (NAACP) objected to the hero of the movie *Superfly*, who was a cocaine dealer. "We must insist," said a spokesman, "that our children are not constantly exposed to a steady diet of

Richard Roundtree as "Shaft," a black private eye who was the equivalent of a street-smart James Bond.

so-called black films that glorify black males as pimps, pushers, gangsters and super males with vast physical prowess, but no cognitive skills."[133]

The Best Movie of the Decade

There were several movies made in the '70s that were based on very popular books. One of the top-selling books of the 1960s was a book by then-unknown author Mario Puzo, called *The Godfather*, a story of a New York Mafia family. In 1970 filming began for the movie version, directed by Francis Ford Coppola. *The Godfather*, according to many critics, was the best movie of the decade—and some earnestly maintain, of all time.

The film starred Marlon Brando as Don Vito Corleone, the head of the crime family, with James Caan, Robert Duvall, and newcomer Al Pacino. It was shot on location in New York, and there were rumors almost immediately after shooting began that the crew was meeting with lots of opposition by local Italians, angry that Hollywood was making a movie insulting to them.

In a turn of events that stunned many people, the producers made a deal with the Italian-American Civil Rights League in New York, which was headed by the son of Mafia boss Joe Columbo. The terms of the deal prohibited the movie producers from using the word "Mafia" in the

movie, and in return, the league would provide access to all New York locations, as well as Italian-looking extras for the film. And as an extra perk, some of the cast got a chance to soak up realism by hanging around true-life mobsters. As one source reports, "[James Caan] was seen so often in the company of Carmine "The Snake" Persico that the local FBI had begun to tail him as an up-and-coming hit man."[134]

Upon its release, *The Godfather* was heralded by critics not only as a masterpiece, but a true blockbuster—something Hollywood had not seen in years. *Newsweek* said, "It promises to be the *Gone With the Wind* of gangster

Al Pacino, Marlon Brando, James Caan, and John Cazale appear in Francis Ford Coppola's hit, The Godfather. *Many critics still claim the movie was the best ever made.*

An Oscar Refusal

The 1970s was a time when some Oscar-winning actors and actresses used the Academy Awards ceremonies as an opportunity to make political statements. One of the first to use the Oscar presentations this way was Marlon Brando, who won Best Actor in 1972, for the movie The Godfather. *In their book* Inside Oscar: The Unofficial History of the Academy Awards, *Mason Wiley and Damien Bona relate how he refused the award, in a very public way.*

Sacheen Littlefeather refuses to accept the Academy Award nominated to Marlon Brando for his role in the movie, The Godfather. Brando and Littlefeather used the opportunity to protest the treatment of Native Americans by the U.S. government.

"It was time for the Best Actor Award. Liv Ullmann and Roger Moore opened the envelope, and the winner was Marlon Brando. The young woman in Native American costume came to the podium, but she brushed away Roger Moore as he tried to hand her the Oscar. She turned to the audience and said:

Hello. My name is Sacheen Littlefeather. I'm Apache and I am president of the National Native American Affirmative Image Committee. I'm representing Marlon Brando this evening and he has asked me to tell you in a very long speech which I cannot share with you presently because of time, but I will be glad to share with the press afterwards that he very regretfully cannot accept this very generous award. And the reasons for this being are the treatment of American Indians today by the film industry. [Some rumbling in the audi-ence.] Excuse me . . . [boos and claps] and on television in movie reruns and also with the recent happenings at Wounded Knee.

I beg at this time that I have not intruded upon this evening and that we will, in the future, in our hearts and our understanding meet with love and generosity.

Thank you on behalf of Marlon Brando.

Nobody booed as Littlefeather went off to the pressroom to read Brando's statement to any members of the press who cared to listen. Those in the audience sat motionless, stunned by what had transpired."

movies."[135] The prediction was correct; *The Godfather* quickly passed *Gone With the Wind* for the number-one position on the all-time box office list.

Horrifying Special Effects

The mid-1970s were a difficult time for many Americans. By 1975 it was clear that the war in Vietnam was lost. The economy was in a major slump, the deepest since the Great Depression of the 1930s. Perhaps because of the somber national mood, escapist movies, rather than relevant ones, were popular.

There were 1970s horror films as well that broke new ground with terrifying special effects. Different from films of earlier decades that concentrated on aliens or monsters like Frankenstein and Wolfman, these movies concerned themselves more with the idea of evil—in all its forms.

The most successful horror film was *The Exorcist,* the story of a twelve-year-old named Regan who is possessed by the devil. Based on a novel by William Peter Blatty that describes a true story that occurred in 1949, the movie was considered one of the most scary films ever produced. Some theatergoers were so terrified that they suffered heart attacks.

The special effects were grotesque—the child vomits forcefully (a combination of oatmeal and pea soup) and rotates her head in a complete circle. Regan's voice is dubbed by a deep-voiced actress, and utters such vile obscenities that many thought the film should have had an X rating. Even so, *The Exorcist* did extremely well at the box office; it was considered a dream come true for Warners, the studio that made the picture, for it broke house records in every theater it played. It was nominated for best picture at the Academy Awards, only narrowly losing to a Robert Redford movie, *The Sting,* in 1973. And the movie so frightened people, one source notes, that "the Catholic Church reported an unprecedented number of requests for exorcisms by people merely quaking with paranoia."[136]

Blockbusters

One of the most popular of these new escapist films was *Jaws,* based on the best-selling book by a former speechwriter for Lyndon Johnson, Peter Benchley. *Jaws* was the story of a huge, man-killing shark, and filming the story would be tricky. The director, twenty-seven-year-old Steven Spielberg, shot on location in the Atlantic Ocean, using three mechanical sharks that were nicknamed Bruce. Each cost a whopping $150,000, and made Universal Studios nervous because they continually malfunctioned. As a result, the film took far longer to make, and ran more than twice its original budget. Even so, producers were concerned that the sharks wouldn't look real. "If anybody in the audience laughs at the shark," one Universal official worried, "we're sunk." [137]

They need not have worried, for *Jaws* surpassed even *The Godfather* at the box office. Though many critics criticized Universal for making "nothing more than a creaky, old-fashioned monster picture reminiscent of *Creature from the Black Lagoon*," [138] few moviegoers listened.

The same was true for *Star Wars*, director George Lucas's high-tech science-fiction movie, which premiered in 1977. It bested *Jaws* and every other movie by earning an unheard-of $256 million dollars, and sold another $2.6 billion in *Star Wars* merchandise. Just as they had turned up their noses at *Jaws*, movie critics bemoaned another film that was pure escapism and relied on special effects to entertain. However, that is precisely what the American public wanted; a movie no longer needed to be relevant and thought-provoking to earn money. And Hollywood loved it!

Epilogue

President Ronald Reagan took office in 1981 promising to bring back America's former glory. The notion appealed to American voters, who voted Reagan in with an overwhelming majority vote.

A Final Thought

As the decade of the 1970s neared an end, few Americans had any sense of nostalgia about it. In a parody of the beginning of Charles Dickens's *A Tale of Two Cities*, one 1979 magazine editorial said of the '70s, "It was the worst of times, it was the worst of times," and urged that the decade end right away, "one year early and not a moment too soon."[139]

Judging from the mood at the time, it is not difficult to understand why so many people had negative feelings about the decade that was just ending. The hostage crisis in Iran showed no sign of resolution, and staggering inflation, along with its high unemployment was a source of nervousness for the American people. Government bureaucracy was monstrous, inhibiting progress rather than enabling it.

President Carter was no more reassuring a presence in the White House than Gerald Ford had been; it seemed as though Watergate's rippling effects would be felt for some time. Without the perspective that time can bring, the '70s must have seemed a tremendous disappointment.

As Americans looked towards the 1980s, they were hardly optimistic. At most, they held a hope that things could return to the way they had been decades earlier. In a speech late in 1979, President Carter acknowledged that such a thing was impossible:

The world of 1980 is as different from what it was in 1960 as the world of 1960 was from that of 1940. . . . We have a keener appreciation of limits now, the limits of government, limits on the use of military power abroad, the limits of manipulation . . . [of] a delicate and balanced national environment. . . . And we face centrifugal forces in our society and in our political system— forces of regionalism, forces of ethnicity, of narrow economic interest, of single issue politics— [that] are testing the resiliency of American pluralism and of our ability to govern.[140]

But Carter's assessment differed from the more upbeat, positive one of a presidential candidate, former actor Ronald Reagan. "They say that America has had its day in the sun, that our nation has passed its zenith," Reagan said. "I utterly reject that view. . . . Liberalism is no longer the answer—it is the problem."[141] It would be Reagan's conservative vision, rather than Carter's liberal one, that resounded with the voters as America entered the 1980s.

Notes

Introduction
A Coming of Age

1. Pagan Kennedy, *Platforms: A Microwaved Cultural Chronicle of the 1970s.* New York: St. Martin's Press, 1994, p. 1.
2. Terrence Zech, interviewed by author, St. Paul, MN, February 3, 1998.
3. Peter Knobler and Greg Mitchell, eds., *Very Seventies: A Cultural History of the 1970s from the Pages of Crawdaddy.* New York: Simon and Schuster, 1995, p. 14.
4. Quoted in Kennedy, *Platforms,* p. 4.

Chapter One:
A House Divided: Politics in the Seventies

5. Quoted in Jules Archer, *The Incredible Sixties.* New York: Harcourt Brace Jovanovich, 1986, p. 42.
6. Quoted in Archer, *The Incredible Sixties,* p. 46.
7. Quoted in Stephen E. Ambrose, *Nixon: The Triumph of a Politician 1962–1972.* New York: Simon and Schuster, 1989, p. 142.
8. Quoted in Ambrose, *Nixon,* p. 345.
9. Quoted in Peter N. Carroll, *It Seemed Like Nothing Happened: The Tragedy and Promise of America in the 1970s.* New York: Holt, Rinehart and Winston, 1982, p. 13.
10. Quoted in Ambrose, *Nixon,* p. 351.
11. Terrence Zech, interviewed by author, St. Paul, MN, February 3, 1998.
12. Quoted in Carroll, *It Seemed Like Nothing Happened,* p. 11.
13. Letter quoted in Ambrose, *Nixon,* p. 350.
14. Quoted in Archer, *The Incredible Sixties,* p. 6.
15. Quoted in Jules Archer, *Rage in the Streets: Mob Violence in America.* New York: Browndeer Press, 1994, pp. 111–12.
16. Quoted in Archer, *Rage in the Streets,* p. 114.
17. Quoted in Archer, *Rage in the Streets,* p. 114.
18. Archer, *Rage in the Streets,* p. 114.
19. Quoted in Archer, *The Incredible Sixties,* p. 8.
20. Quoted in Fred Emery, *Watergate: The Corruption of American Politics and the Fall of Richard Nixon.* New York: Times Books, 1994, p. 3.
21. Quoted in Carroll, *It Seemed Like Nothing Happened,* p. 80.

22. Barbara Silberdick Feinberg, *Watergate: Scandal in the White House*. New York: Franklin Watts, 1990, p. 25.

23. Quoted in Sallie G. Randolph, *Richard M. Nixon, President*. New York: Walker, 1989, pp. 107–108.

24. Quoted in Emery, *Watergate*, p. 415.

25. Quoted in Randolph, *Richard M. Nixon*, p. 112.

26. Robert Dallek, *Hail to the Chief: The Making and Unmaking of American Presidents*. New York: Hyperion, 1996, p. 195.

27. Dallek, *Hail to the Chief*, p. 195.

Chapter Two:
"I Am Woman; Hear Me Roar"

28. Jules Archer, *Breaking Barriers: The Feminine Revolution from Susan B. Anthony to Margaret Sanger to Betty Friedan*. New York: Viking, 1991, p. 146.

29. Arthur Stein, *Seeds of the Seventies: Values, Work, and Commitment in Post-Vietnam America*. Hanover, NH: University Press of New England, 1985, p. 11.

30. Quoted in Winifred Wandersee, *On the Move: American Women in the 1970s*. Boston: Twayne Publishers, 1988, p. 2.

31. Quoted in Kennedy, *Platforms*, p. 87.

32. Archer, *Breaking Barriers*, pp. 126–27.

33. Quoted in Curt Smith, *Long Time Gone: The Years of Turmoil Remembered*. South Bend, IN: Icarus Press, 1982, p. 93.

34. Tracy Porter-Moss, interviewed by author, Bloomington, MN, March 19, 1998.

35. Carroll, *It Seemed Like Nothing Happened*, p. 25.

36. Kennedy, *Platforms*, p. 93.

37. Tracy Porter-Moss, interviewed by author, Bloomington, MN, March 19, 1998.

38. Kennedy, *Platforms*, p. 94.

39. Quoted in Kennedy, *Platforms*, p. 94.

40. Quoted in Suzanne Levine and Harriet Lyons, eds., *The Decade of Women: A Ms. History of the Seventies in Words and Pictures*. New York: G. P. Putnam's Sons, 1980, p. 85.

41. Quoted in Carroll, *It Seemed Like Nothing Happened*, p. 31.

42. Quoted in Levine and Lyons, *The Decade of Women*, p. 71.

43. Quoted in Levine and Lyons, *The Decade of Women*, p. 79.

44. Quoted in William H. Chafe, *The Road to Equality: American Women Since 1962*. New York: Oxford University Press, 1994, p. 102.

45. Quoted in Levine and Lyons, *The Decade of Women*, p. 81.

Chapter Three: A Piece of the Pie

46. Carroll, *It Seemed Like Nothing Happened*, p. 39.

47. Quoted in Carroll, *It Seemed Like Nothing Happened*, p. 40.

48. Robin D. G. Kelley, *Into the Fire: African Americans Since 1970*. New York: Oxford University Press, 1996, p. 17.

49. Quoted in Carroll, *It Seemed Like Nothing Happened*, p. 54.

50. Quoted in Mary Hull, *Struggle and Love 1972–1997: From the Gary Convention to the Aftermath of the Million Man March*. Philadelphia: Chelsea House, 1997, pp. 37–38.

51. Quoted in Hull, *Struggle and Love*, p. 21.

52. Quoted in Hull, *Struggle and Love*, p. 21.

53. Quoted in Kennedy, *Platforms*, p. 69.

54. Quoted in Paul Chaat Smith and Robert Allen Warrior, *Like a Hurricane: The Indian Movement from Alcatraz to Wounded Knee*. New York: New Press, 1996, pp. 106–107.

55. Smith and Warrior, *Like a Hurricane*, p. 269.

56. Quoted in Carroll, *It Seemed Like Nothing Happened*, pp. 252–53.

57. Quoted in Carroll, *It Seemed Like Nothing Happened*, p. 255.

58. Quoted in Carroll, *It Seemed Like Nothing Happened*, p. 255.

59. Quoted in Carroll, *It Seemed Like Nothing Happened*, p. 255.

Chapter Four: Energy and the Environment

60. Rachel Carson, *Silent Spring*. New York: Houghton Mifflin, 1962, p. 3.

61. Kirkpatrick Sale, *The Green Revolution: The American Environmental Movement 1962–1992*. New York: Hill and Wang, 1993, p. 25.

62. Kennedy, *Platforms*, pp. 32–33.

63. Marc Mowrey and Tim Redmond, *Not in Our Backyard: The People and Events That Shaped America's Modern Environmental Movement*. New York: William Morrow, 1993, p. 39.

64. Quoted in Mowray and Redmond, *Not in Our Backyard*, p. 42.

65. Quoted in Carroll, *It Seemed Like Nothing Happened*, p. 126.

66. Quoted in Mowray and Redmond, *Not in Our Backyard*, p. 102.

67. Quoted in Kennedy, *Platforms*, p. 40.

68. Quoted in Carroll, *It Seemed Like Nothing Happened*, p. 122.

69. Quoted in Carroll, *It Seemed Like Nothing Happened*, p. 123.

70. Quoted in Carroll, *It Seemed Like Nothing Happened*, p. 123.

71. Quoted in Carroll, *It Seemed Like Nothing Happened*, p. 122.

72. Quoted in Kennedy, *Platforms*, p. 41.

73. Quoted in Carroll, *It Seemed Like Nothing Happened*, p. 122.

74. Irene Kiefer, *Nuclear Energy at the Crossroads*. New York: Atheneum,

1982, pp. 51–52.

75. Quoted in Carroll, *It Seemed Like Nothing Happened*, p. 218.

76. Quoted in Laurence Pringle, *Nuclear Energy: Troubled Past, Uncertain Future*. New York: Macmillan, 1989, p. 39.

Chapter Five:
"No Rules" Rule: Fashion and
Fads in the Seventies

77. Quoted in Frank W. Hoffmann and William G. Bailey, *Fashion & Merchandising Fads*. New York: Haworth Press, 1994, p. 156.

78. Quoted in Hoffmann and Bailey, *Fashion & Merchandising Fads*, p. 157.

79. Charles Panati, *Panati's Parade of Fads, Follies, and Manias*. New York: Harper, 1991. p. 369.

80. Quoted in Fashion '71: Anything Goes," *Newsweek*, March 29, 1971, p. 68.

81. Quoted in "Fashion '71," *Newsweek*, p. 75.

82. Quoted in "Hot Pants: Legs are Back," *Time*, February 1, 1971, p. 48.

83. Maggie Paxton Murray, *Changing Styles in Fashion: Who, What, Why*. New York: Fairchild Publications, 1989, pp. 115–16.

84. David Bond, *The Guinness Guide to 20th Century Fashion*. Middlesex, England: Guinness Publishing,

1988, p. 194.

85. Panati, *Panati's Parade*, p. 369.

86. Jane Stern and Michael Stern, *The Encyclopedia of Bad Taste*. New York: HarperCollins, 1990, p. 184.

87. Stern, *Encyclopedia of Bad Taste*, p. 183.

88. Stern, *Encyclopedia of Bad Taste*, p. 184.

89. Quoted in Stern, *Encyclopedia of Bad Taste*, p. 166.

90. Stern, *Encyclopedia of Bad Taste*, p. 165.

91. Stern, *Encyclopedia of Bad Taste*, p. 94.

92. Bond, *The Guinness Guide to 20th Century Fashion*, p. 200.

93. Andrew J. Edelstein and Kevin McDonough, *The Seventies: From Hot Pants to Hot Tubs*. New York: Dutton, 1990, p. 116.

94. Edelstein and McDonough, *The Seventies*, p. 117.

Chapter Six:
Music of the Seventies

95. Joe Stuessy, *Rock & Roll: Its History and Stylistic Development*. Englewood Cliffs, NJ: Prentice Hall, 1990, p. 302.

96. Edelstein and McDonough, *The Seventies*, p. 134.

97. Ed Ward, Geoffrey Stokes, and Ken Tucker, *Rock of Ages: The Rolling Stone History of Rock &*

Roll, New York: Summit, 1986, p. 468.

98. Ward, Stokes, and Tucker, *Rock of Ages*, p. 468.

99. Stuessy, *Rock & Roll*, p. 467.

100. Quoted in Timothy White, *Rock Lives: Profiles and Interviews*. New York: Henry Holt, 1990, p. 402.

101. Quoted in Edelstein and McDonough, *The Seventies*, p. 160.

102. Edelstein and McDonough, *The Seventies*, p. 160.

103. Ward, Stokes, and Tucker, *Rock of Ages*, p. 474.

104. Quoted in Edelstein and McDonough, *The Seventies*, p. 142.

105. Ward, Stokes, and Tucker, *Rock of Ages*, p. 475.

106. Stuessy, *Rock & Roll*, p. 306.

107. Edelstein and McDonough, *The Seventies*, p. 152.

108. Quoted in White, *Rock Lives*, p. 287.

109. Ward, Stokes, and Tucker, *Rock of Ages*, p. 547.

110. Stuessy, *Rock & Roll*, p. 312.

111. Quoted in Ward, Stokes, and Tucker, *Rock of Ages*, p. 557.

112. Quoted in Edelstein and McDonough, *The Seventies*, p. 180.

113. Edelstein and McDonough, *The Seventies*, p. 174.

114. Edelstein and McDonough, *The Seventies*, p. 174.

Chapter Seven: Television and Film in the Seventies

115. Edelstein and McDonough, *The Seventies*, p. 183.

116. Quoted in Steven D. Stark, *Glued to the Set: The 60 Television Shows and Events That Made Us Who We Are Today*. New York: Free Press, 1997, p. 163.

117. Donna McCrohan, *Prime Time, Our Time: America's Life and Times Through the Prism of Television*. Rocklin, CA: Prima Publishing, 1990, p. 210.

118. Quoted in McCrohan, *Prime Time*, p. 208.

119. Quoted in Erik Barnouw, *Tube of Plenty: The Evolution of American Television*. New York: Oxford University Press, 1990, p. 433.

120. Stark, *Glued to the Set*, p. 168.

121. Stark, *Glued to the Set*, pp. 169–70.

122. Edelstein and McDonough, *The Seventies*, p. 188.

123. McCrohan, *Prime Time, Our Time*, p. 215.

124. Jane Stern and Michael Stern, *Encyclopedia of Pop Culture: An A to Z Guide of Who's Who from Aerobics and Bubble Gum to Valley of the Dolls and Moon Unit Zappa*. New York: HarperCollins, 1992, p. 436.

125. Quoted in Stark, *Glued to the Set*, p. 196.

126. Quoted in Stark, *Glued to the Set,* p. 200.
127. Edelstein and McDonough, *The Seventies*, pp. 192–93.
128. Quoted in Stark, *Glued to the Set,* p. 201.
129. Mark A. Reid, *Redefining Black Film.* Berkeley: University of California Press, 1993, p. 77.
130. Quoted in Reid, *Redefining Black Film*, p. 84.
131. Quoted in Edelstein and McDonough, *The Seventies*, p. 5.
132. Quoted in Edelstein and McDonough, *The Seventies*, p. 6.
133. Quoted in Edelstein and McDonough, *The Seventies*, p. 6.
134. Edelstein and McDonough, *The Seventies*, p. 19.
135. Quoted in Mason Wiley and Damien Bona, *Inside Oscar: The Unofficial History of the Academy Awards.* New York: Ballantine, 1986, p. 469.
136. Edelstein and McDonough, *The Seventies*, p. 19.
137. Panati, *Panati's Parade*, p. 410.
138. Quoted in Wiley and Bona, *Inside Oscar*, p. 511.

**Epilogue:
A Final Thought**

139. Quoted in Carroll, *It Seemed Like Nothing Happened*, p. ix.
140. Quoted in Carroll, *It Seemed Like Nothing Happened*, p. 339.
141. Quoted in Carroll, *It Seemed Like Nothing Happened*, p. 340.

Chronology

1970

January 3: Beatles record "I, Me Mine," their last song together.

April 1: Major offensive launched by North Vietnamese.

April 22: First Earth Day celebrated.

April 30: Nixon orders thirty thousand U.S. troops sent into Cambodia.

May 4: Four Kent State students shot during antiwar protest.

September 28: Egyptian president Nasser dies of heart attack. Anwar Sadat succeeds him.

1971

January 18: George McGovern announces he'll run for president in 1972.

April 25: Bangladesh announces independence from Pakistan.

June 27: More than five thousand demonstrate for gay rights in New York.

September 11: Former Soviet leader Nikita Krushchev dies.

December 26: Pentagon announces the heaviest bombing of North Vietnam since 1968.

1972

January 16: American religious leaders call for an end to the war in Vietnam.

February 21: Nixon leaves for historic eight-day trip to China.

March 15: *The Godfather* released.

April 17: First women race in the Boston Marathon.

May 2: Nixon becomes the first U.S. president to visit Moscow; he signs a nuclear arms treaty.

June 6: McGovern clinches Democratic presidential nomination.

June 17: Break-in at Watergate offices of Democratic headquarters.

September 5–6: Palestinian terrorists kill two Israeli athletes and kidnap nine at Olympics in Munich.

November 7: Nixon defeats McGovern in election.

1973

January 22: Supreme Court decision in *Roe v. Wade* legalizes abortion.

February 27: Native American activists take hostages at Wounded Knee, South Dakota.

May 17: Senate Watergate hearings begin.

October 2: Nixon orders rationing of heating oil.

October 10: Vice President Spiro Agnew resigns.

1974

February 6: House of Representatives votes to begin impeachment proceedings against Nixon.

April 8: Hank Aaron beats Babe Ruth's home run record.

June 12: Little League of America allows girls to play for the first time.

June 20: David Bowie's *Ziggy Stardust* album wins Gold Record.

August 8: Nixon announces resignation.

August 9: Gerald Ford sworn in as president.

September 12: Racial rioting in Boston over forced busing.

1975

April 1: Employment at highest (8.7 percent) since the depression.

April 19: Disco getting big with "The Hustle" on the charts.

April 29: President Ford orders total evacuation of South Vietnam.

September 5: Assassination attempt on President Ford.

September 30: Home Box Office (HBO) begins programming.

October 11: Premier of *Saturday Night Live*.

1976

January 31: Pope Paul VI speaks out against feminism.

February 18: Environmental Protection Agency bans mercury pesticides.

June 8: Jimmy Carter clinches Democratic presidential nomination.

July 4: America celebrates its bicentennial.

November 4: Carter elected.

1977

May 13: Five hundred people arrested in nuclear protest in New Hampshire.

July 29: *Women's Wear Daily* reports "punk" style is highly popular.

August 16: Elvis Presley dies.

November 19: *Star Wars* becomes top-grossing film ever.

December 14: *Saturday Night Fever* released.

1978

July 25: First test tube baby born in England.

August 15: House of Representatives extends deadline for ratification of Equal Rights Amendment (ERA) until 1982.

September 17: Camp David meetings result in Egypt-Israel peace accords.

1979

March 28: Nuclear leak at Three Mile Island confirmed.

May 1: George Bush announces his bid for presidency.

June 20: Gas rationing throughout United States because of shortage.

November 4: Iranian students seize hostages at U.S. embassy in Tehran.

For Further Reading

Paul Buhle, ed., *Popular Culture in America*. Minneapolis: University of Minnesota Press, 1987. Good section on television and film.

Michael Cader, ed., *Saturday Night Live: The First Twenty Years*. New York: Houghton Mifflin, 1994. Excellent photographs and background of show.

Christopher Paul Denis and Michael Denis, *Favorite Families on TV*. New York: Citadel Press, 1992. Good section on *All in the Family*.

E. B. Fincher, *The Vietnam War*. New York: Franklin Watts, 1980. Easy-to-read information on the roots of the U.S. involvement in Vietnam.

Jay S. Harris, ed., *TV Guide: The First 25 Years*. New York: Simon and Schuster, 1978. Good article about children's programming in the 1970s.

James Haskins and Kathleen Benson, *The 60s Reader*, New York: Viking Kestrel, 1989. Helpful background material, especially regarding the Black Power movement.

Charles Kaiser, *1968 in America*. New York: Weidenfeld and Nicolson, 1988. Helpful background for social unrest of the 1970s.

Deborah Kent, *The Vietnam War: "What Are We Fighting For?"* Springfield, NJ: Enslow, 1994. Easy to read, good background on war.

Kim McQuaid, *The Anxious Years: America in the Vietnam-Watergate Era*. New York: Basic Books, 1989. Good section on polarization of Americans in the early 1970s.

Milton Meltzer, *The American Promise: Voices of a Changing Nation 1945–Present*. New York: Bantam, 1990. Good background material on antiwar movement.

Isobel V. Morin, *Impeaching the President*. Brookfield, CT: Millbrook Press, 1996. Excellent glossary and index, as well as helpful information on the impeachment articles brought against Nixon.

Judith Papachristou, *Women Together: A History in Documents of the Women's Movement in the United States*. New York: Alfred A. Knopf, 1976. Good information on early radical feminist organizations.

Elaine Pascoe, *Racial Prejudice: Why We Can't Overcome*. New York: Franklin Watts, 1985. Good overview of civil rights activity in the 1970s.

Theodore H. White, *Breach of Faith: The Fall of Richard Nixon.* New York: Atheneum Publishers, 1975. Excellent appendices and index.

Michael Winship, *Television.* New York: Random House, 1998. Helpful information about sports reporting in the 1970s.

Robin Wood, *Hollywood from Vietnam to Reagan.* New York: Columbia University Press, 1986. Interesting chapter on horror movies in the 1970s.

Works Consulted

Stephen E. Ambrose, *Nixon: The Triumph of a Politician 1962–1972*. New York: Simon and Schuster, 1989. Excellent index; helpful information about Watergate cover-up.

Jules Archer, *Breaking Barriers: The Feminist Revolution from Susan B. Anthony to Margaret Sanger to Betty Friedan*. New York: Viking, 1991. Helpful information on women's dissatisfaction in the early 1970s.

———, *The Incredible Sixties*. New York: Harcourt Brace Jovanovich, 1986. Readable account of what provided the background of the politics of the 1970s.

———, *Rage in the Streets: Mob Violence in America*. New York: Browndeer Press, 1994. Excellent section on aftermath of Kent State.

Erik Barnouw, *Tube of Plenty: The Evolution of American Television*. New York: Oxford University Press, 1990. Helpful index.

David Bond, *The Guinness Guide to 20th Century Fashion*. Middlesex, England: Guinness Publishing, 1988. Good background on the denim craze, as well as hairstyles of the 1970s.

Victor Bondi, ed. *American Decades: 1970–1979*. Detroit: Gale Research, 1995. Excellent material on the Watergate scandal.

Peter N. Carroll, *It Seemed Like Nothing Happened: The Tragedy and Promise of America in the 1970s*. New York: Holt, Rinehart and Winston, 1982. Excellent notes and index.

Rachel Carson, *Silent Spring*. New York: Houghton Mifflin, 1962. Invaluable background source.

William H. Chafe, *The Road to Equality: American Women Since 1962*. New York: Oxford University Press, 1994. Excellent chronology.

Robert Dallek, *Hail to the Chief: The Making and Unmaking of American Presidents*. New York: Hyperion, 1996. Helpful index and source notes.

Clifton Daniel, ed. *Chronicle of America*. New York: DK Publishers, 1997. Helpful year-by-year headlines of the 1970s.

Andrew J. Edelstein and Kevin McDonough, *The Seventies: From Hot Pants to Hot Tubs*. New York: Dutton, 1990. Very helpful material on 1970s television and fashion.

Fred Emery, *Watergate: The Corruption of American Politics and the Fall of*

Richard Nixon. New York: Times Books, 1994. Excellent notes.

Barbara Silberdick Feinberg, *Watergate: Scandal in the White House.* New York: Franklin Watts, 1990. Readable; good notes.

Frank W. Hoffmann and William G. Bailey, *Fashion & Merchandising Fads.* New York: Haworth Press, 1994. Excellent background on blue jeans and the midi.

Mary Hull, *Struggle and Love 1972–1997: From the Gary Convention to the Aftermath of the Million Man March.* Philadelphia: Chelsea House, 1997. Excellent section on busing and affirmative action in the 1970s.

Robin D. G. Kelley, *Into the Fire: African Americans Since 1970.* New York: Oxford University Press, 1996. Excellent bibliography; good information on the black middle class in the 1970s.

Pagan Kennedy, *Platforms: A Microwaved Cultural Chronicle of the 1970s.* New York: St. Martin's Press, 1994. Very helpful for teenage perspective of life in the 1970s.

Irene Kiefer, *Nuclear Energy at the Crossroads.* New York: Atheneum, 1982. Excellent background material on dangers of nuclear power.

Peter Knobler and Greg Mitchell, eds., *Very Seventies: A Cultural History of the 1970s from the Pages of Crawdaddy.* New York: Simon and Schuster, 1995. Helpful information on music of the 1970s.

Suzanne Levine and Harriet Lyons, eds., *The Decade of Women: A Ms. History of the Seventies in Words and Pictures.* New York: G. P. Putnam's Sons, 1980. Helpful auxiliary material on the ERA.

Andrew Marum and Frank Parise, *Follies and Foibles: A View of 20th Century Fads.* New York: Facts On File, 1984. Excellent section on fashion accessories of the 1970s.

Donna McCrohan, *Prime Time, Our Time: America's Life and Times Through the Prism of Television.* Rocklin, CA: Prima Publishing, 1990. Excellent section on nostalgia television of the late 1970s.

Marc Mowrey and Tim Redmond, *Not in Our Backyard: The People and Events That Shaped America's Modern Environmental Movement.* New York: William Morrow, 1993. Excellent index; good background material on Earth Day 1970.

Maggie Paxton Murray, *Changing Styles in Fashion: Who, What, Why.* New York: Fairchild Publications, 1989. Good information on the miniskirt.

Newsweek, "Fashion '71: Anything Goes," March 29, 1971.

Charles Panati, *Panati's Parade of Fads,*

Follies, and Manias. New York: Harper, 1991. Very readable background on fashion and movies of the decade.

Tracy Porter-Moss, interviewed by author, Bloomington, MN, March 19, 1998.

Laurence Pringle, *Nuclear Energy: Troubled Past, Uncertain Future*. New York: Macmillan, 1989. Good background information on building of nuclear power plants in the 1970s.

Sallie G. Randolf, *Richard M. Nixon, President*. New York: Walker, 1989. Easy reading, good quotes.

Mark A. Reid, *Redefining Black Film*. Berkeley: University of California Press, 1993. Good section on black adventure films of the 1970s.

Kirkpatrick Sale, *The Green Revolution: The American Environmental Movement 1962–1992*. New York: Hill and Wang, 1993. Very readable summary of 1970s environmental activity.

Curt Smith, *Long Time Gone: The Years of Turmoil Remembered*. South Bend, IN: Icarus Press, 1982. Good interviews with key personalities of the 1970s.

Paul Chaat Smith and Robert Allen Warrior, *Like a Hurricane: The Indian Movement from Alcatraz to Wounded Knee*. New York: New Press, 1996. Excellent background on the Amer-

ican Indian Movement.

Steven D. Stark, *Glued to the Set: The 60 Television Shows and Events That Made Us Who We Are Today*. New York: Free Press, 1997. Helpful information on 1970s sitcoms.

Arthur Stein, *Seeds of the Seventies: Values, Work, and Commitment in Post-Vietnam America*. Hanover, NH: University Press of New England, 1985. Excellent bibliography.

Jane Stern and Michael Stern, *The Encyclopedia of Bad Taste*. New York: HarperCollins, 1990. Highly readable, good photographs.

———, *Encyclopedia of Pop Culture: An A to Z Guide of Who's Who from Aerobics and Bubble Gum to Valley of the Dolls and Moon Unit Zappa*. New York: HarperCollins, 1992. Easily browsed, interesting information on 1970s fads.

Joe Stuessy, *Rock & Roll: Its History and Stylistic Development*. Englewood Cliffs, NJ: Prentice Hall, 1990. Helpful information on post-Beatles rock groups.

Time, "Hot Pants: Legs Are Back," February 1, 1971.

Winifred D. Wandersee, *On the Move: American Women in the 1970s*. Boston: Twayne Publishers, 1988. Excellent index and notes.

Ed Ward, Geoffrey Stokes, and Ken Tucker, *Rock of Ages: The Rolling*

Stone History of Rock & Roll. New York: Summit, 1986. Good information on heavy metal groups.

Timothy White, *Rock Lives: Profiles and Interviews.* New York: Henry Holt, 1990. Excellent primary quotes from rock stars of the 1970s.

Mason Wiley and Damien Bona, *Inside Oscar: The Unofficial History of the Academy Awards.* New York: Ballantine, 1986. Fascinating reading, good background on *Jaws* and *The Godfather.*

Terrence Zech, interviewed by author, St. Paul, MN, February 3, 1998.

Index

abortion, 30
Academy Awards, 104, 105
advertising, 27–29, 72
affirmative action, 43
African Americans. *See* blacks
Agent Orange, 13
Agnew, Spiro, 13, 21
Akroyd, Dan, 96, 97
Alcatraz Island, 43–44
All in the Family, 90–93, 94, 95, 100
American Decades: 1970–1979 (Bondi), 12
American Indian Movement (AIM), 44, 45
Anheuser-Busch Brewery, 72
Annie Hall, 67
antiwar movement, 10, 11–14, 17, 25
Archer, Jules, 16
attitudes
  about Bicentennial celebration, 22
  of 1960s, 5–6, 90
  of 1970s, 7, 15, 17, 90, 100, 107–108
  as portrayed on television, 89–90, 100
  about Vietnamese War, 10, 11–16, 17
  about women, 24, 25, 27, 30, 32, 34–35

Bakke, Allan, 43
Beatles, 7, 76–77, 82
Bee Gees, 86
Begin, Menachim, 22
Belushi, John, 96, 97
Bernstein, Carl, 20
Bicentennial celebration, 22
Black Caesar, 101
Black Liberation Front, 37
Black Panthers, 37, 39
blacks

affirmative action and, 43
civil rights movement and, 36–39, 41–42
education and, 36, 39–41
during 1960s, 36–37
as portrayed in movies, 101–103
as portrayed on television, 90, 95–96, 98–100
voting and, 42
blaxploitation films, 101–103
Blondie, 85
Blues Brothers, 97
Bombeck, Erma, 34
Bona, Damien, 104
Bondi, Victor, 12
Boston, 39–40
Bowie, David, 79–80
Brando, Marlon, 103, 104
Brennan, Peter, 16
Brezhnev, Leonid, 17
Brown, H. Rap, 36–37
Brown v. Board of Education, 36
busing, 39–40

Cambodia, 11–13, 18
Camp David accords, 22–23
Carmichael, Stokely, 36–37
"Carolina in My Mind" (Taylor), 80
Carroll, Peter
  on Bicentennal celebration, 22
  on sexual revolution, 27
Carson, Rachel, 49–50
Carter, Jimmy, 23
  election of 1980 and, 107, 108
  Love Canal and, 61–62
  Middle East peace treaty and, 22
  music and, 82
Chase, Chevy, 96, 97
China, 17, 19

Civil Rights Act of 1964, 32
civil rights movement
  of blacks, 36–39, 41–42
  of Native Americans, 43–48
  of women, 25–26, 29–30, 32–33
clothing
  bikinis, 74
  economy and, 64
  jeans, 71–72, 74–75
  pants, 65–67
  shoes, 67–68, 70
  skirts, 63–64
  suits, 68–70
  T-shirts, 72
Committee to Re-Elect the President (CREEP), 19
Coneheads, 97
Consumer Reports, 67
contraceptives, 27
Coppola, Francis Ford, 103
Counter Intelligence Program (COINTELPRO), 38
Court, Margaret, 28
Cox, Archibald, 43
Cronkite, Walter, 57

Dahl, Gary, 70
Daily News, 79
daylight savings time, 54
DDT, 52
Dean, John, 20–21
demonstrations, 10, 13–16
Denis, Christopher and Michael, 92
dioxin (TCDD), 61
disco (music), 86–88
divorce, 15

Earth Day, 51–52, 68
Edelstein, Andrew J.
  on disco music, 86–87
  on Led Zeppelin, 82
  on youth and television, 90

education
 of blacks, 36, 39–41
 women and, 32–33
Educational Amendments Act,
 32–33
Egypt, 22
Eisenhower, Dwight David, 9
elections
 of 1968, 37
 of 1972, 18–19
 of 1976, 22
 of 1980, 107, 108
Ellsberg, Daniel, 12
The Encyclopedia of Bad Taste
 (Stern), 72
Encyclopedia of Pop Culture
 (Stern), 97
energy
 crisis, 46–48, 53–56
 sources of
  nuclear, 57–59
  oil, 53–56
  other, 46–48
environmental movement, ,
 49–52, 56
 Earth Day, 51–52
 Love Canal, 59–62
 Three Mile Island, 57–59
Equal Employment
 Opportunity Commission,
 32
Equal Rights Amendment
 (ERA), 33–35
Ervin, Sam, 20–21
The Exorcist, 105

FADD (Fight Against Dictating
 Designers), 64
Falwell, Jerry, 34
Favorite Families on TV
 (Denis), 92
Federal Bureau of
 Investigation (FBI), 37, 38
The Feminine Mystique
 (Friedan), 25
feminism, 25–27, 31, 33–35
"Fire and Rain" (Taylor), 80
folk music, 80
Follies and Foibles: A View of

20th Century Fads (Marum
 and Parise), 64, 74
Ford, Gerald, 21–22, 96, 97
Foxx, Redd, 96
Friedan, Betty, 25, 26–27

GAMS (Girls/Guys Against
 More Skirt), 64
gasoline, 54–56
Gasparro, Frank, 16
glam rock, 78–80
glitter rock, 78–80
The Godfather, 103–105, 106
"God Save the Queen (She
 Ain't a Human Being)"
 (Rotten), 86
Good Times, 95–96
Greenpeace, 50
Greider, William, 100

hairstyles, 79
Haley, Alex, 98, 99
Happy Days, 100–101
Harry, Debbie, 85
Hatcher, Richard, 42
Hayes, Denis, 52
health movement, 69
heavy metal (music), 81–83
Hickle, Walter, 52
Hooker Chemical Company,
 61
Hoover, J. Edgar, 37
Houses of the Holy (Led
 Zeppelin), 82
Hues Corporation, 86

"I Feel the Earth Move"
 (King), 81
Indians. See Native Americans
inflation, 107
Inside Oscar: The Unofficial
 History of the Academy
 Awards (Wiley and Bona),
 104
Israel, 22, 53
Italian-American Civil Rights
 League, 103
It Seemed Like Nothing
 Happened: The Tragedy and

Promise of America in the
 1970s (Carroll), 22
"Its Too Late" (King), 81

Jackson, Jesse, 42
Jaws, 105–106
The Jeffersons, 95, 96
jewelry, 64, 71
Johnson, Lyndon, 9–10, 32
Jordache, 74

Kalso, Anne, 68
Kennedy, John F., 9
Kennedy, Pagan, 54
Kennedy, Ted, 12
Kent State University, 13–15
King, Billie Jean, 28
King, Carole, 80–81
King, Martin Luther, Jr., 37, 41
Kissinger, Henry, 17
Knobler, Peter, 6–7

Landon, Michael, 100
Lear, Norman, 91, 93, 95, 96
Led Zeppelin, 81–82
Lieberman, Nancy, 32–33
Little House on the Prairie, 100
Louisville (KY), 39
Love Canal, 59–62
Lucas, George, 106

Mafia, 103
Malcolm X, 41
Manson, Charles, 19
Marshall, Thurgood, 43
Martin, Steve, 97
Marum, Andrew
 on bikinis, 74
 on jewelry fads, 64
The Mary Tyler Moore Show,
 93–95
Masterpiece Theatre, 98
McCord, James, 19, 20
McCrae, George, 86
McDonough, Kevin
 on disco music, 86–87
 on Led Zeppelin, 82
 on youth and television, 90
McGovern, George, 18–19, 20

Means, LaNada, 43–44
Me Decade, 15
mellow music, 80–81
Michaels, Lorne, 96, 98
Middle East peace treaty, 22
Mitchell, Greg, 6–7
The Mod Squad, 90
mood rings, 71
Moore, Mary Tyler, 93
movies, 5, 101–106
Mowrey, Marc, 52
Murray, Bill, 97, 98

Naisbitt, John, 78
National Association for the
   Advancement of Colored
   People (NAACP), 102–103
National Black Political
   Assembly, 41–42
National Guard, 13, 14
National Organization for
   Women (NOW), 32, 33
Native Americans
   activism of, 43–44, 45, 47
   courts and, 44, 46–47, 48
   living conditions of, 42–43
Nelson, Gaylord, 51
Newsweek, 86, 103, 105
New York City, 15–16, 26
New York Dolls, 83
New York Times, 12, 17, 21,
   101–102
Nixon Richard
   becomes president, 10–11
   blacks and, 37, 38
   on employment of women,
   32
   on energy crisis, 53, 56
   environment and, 52–53
   on importance of Vietnamese
   War, 11
   on Kent State incident, 15
   on nuclear power, 57
   pardon of, 22
   Pentagon Papers and, 12
   on relations with Soviet
   Union, 18
   resignation of, 21
   on SST, 53

taped conversations of, 21
trip to China, 17, 18
trip to Soviet Union, 17–18
Vietnamese War and, 11, 13,
   17
Watergate and, 19–20
*Not in Our Backyard: The
People and Events That Shaped
America's Modern
Environmental Movement*
(Mowrey and Redmond), 60
Novello, Don, 97
nuclear power, 57–59
nuclear testing, 50

Oglala Sioux Reservation, 44,
   45
oil
   alternatives to, 56–59
   environment and, 52
   gasoline, 54–56
   production of, 52, 53
Organization of Petroleum
   Exporting Countries
   (OPEC), 53
ozone layer, 53

*Panati's Parade of Fads, Follies,
   and Manias* (Panati), 70
Parise, Frank
   on bikinis, 74
   on jewelry fads, 64
Pentagon Papers, 12
pesticides, 49, 52, 61
pet rocks, 70
Physical Graffiti (Led
   Zeppelin), 82
the pill, 27
*Platforms: A Microwaved
   Cultural Chronicle of the 1970s*
   (Kennedy), 54
plumbers unit, 12
polyester, 68, 70
President's Advisory
   Commission on Civil
   Disorders, 37
Project Independence, 56
punk rock, 83–86

radio, 78
Radner, Gilda, 97
Ramones, 83
Reagan, Ronald, 108
Redford, Robert, 105
Redmond, Tim, 52
religion, 92
Reynolds, Joshua, 71
Rhodes, James, 13–14
Richards, Keith, 83
Rich Man, Poor Man, 98, 100
Riggs, Bobby, 28
"Rip Her to Shreds," 85
Rock, John, 27
rock music, 76–80, 81–86, 89
*Rock & Roll: Its History and
   Stylistic Development*
   (Stuessy), 78
"Rock the Boat," 86
"Rock Your Baby," 86
Roe v. Wade, 30
The Rookies, 90
Roots, 98–100
Rostow, Walt, 10
Rotten, Johnny, 83–84, 86

Sadat, Anwar, 22
Sanford and Son, 95, 96
Saturday Night Fever, 5, 86,
   87–88
Saturday Night Live, 96–98
Schlafly, Phyllis, 34–35
seals, 50
*The Seventies: From Hot Pants
   to Hot Tubs* (Edelstein and
   McDonough), 82
Sex Pistols, 83–84, 86
sexual revolution, 27
Shaft, 101
Silent Spring (Carson), 49–50
Smith, Patti, 85
Smith, Paul Chaat, 44
Soviet Union, 17–18
Spielberg, Steven, 105
sports, 28, 32–33
Sports Illustrated, 69
"Stairway to Heaven," 81
Stapleton, Jean, 93
Stardust, Ziggy, 80

Star Wars, 106
Stern, Jane and Michael
  on clothing styles, 72
  on *Saturday Night Live*, 97
  on warm-up suits, 70
The Sting, 105
Straus, Levi, 71
streaking, 72–74
Student Nonviolent
  Coordinating Committee
  (SNCC), 25
Stuessy, Joe, 78
Summer, Donna, 86
Superfly, 101, 102–103
supersonic transport (SST), 53
Susan B. Anthony dollar, 16
"Sweet Baby James" (Taylor),
  80
*Sweet Sweetback's Baadasssss
  Song,* 101

Tapestry (King), 81
Tate, Sharon, 19
Taylor, James, 80
televisioin
  blacks as portrayed on, 90,
  95–96, 98–100
  deals with issues/as mirror of
  society, 89–90, 100
  sitcoms, 90–96
  variety shows, 96–98
  development of miniseries,
  98–100
  Vietnamese War and, 12,
  16–17
  women as portrayed on,
  93–95
  youth and, 90, 94, 96, 98
Thomas, Richard, 100
Thornburgh, Richard, 58,
  59

Three Mile Island, 57–59
Time, 51, 80, 94
Title IX, 32–33
toxic waste, 59–62
Travolta, John, 5, 87
Trouble Man, 101
Truman, Harry, 9

United States
  Congress
    House of Representatives
      Judiciary Commitee, 21
    Senate Select Committee on
      Presidential Campaign
      Activities, 20–21
  Constitution, 30, 33–35
  Justice Department Law
    Enforcement Assistance
    Administration, 37–38
  Supreme Court
    Bakke decision, 43
    Brown v. Board of Education,
      36
    Manson case and, 19
    Pentagon Papers decision,
      12
    Roe v. Wade, 30
University of California, 43
Upstairs, Downstairs, 98

*Very Seventies: A Cultural
  History of the 1970s from the
  Pages of Crawdaddy* (Knobler
  and Mitchell), 6–7
Vietnamese War
  beginnings of, 9
  effect of, 8
  expansion of, 9, 11–13, 18
  importance of, 9, 11
  Johnson and, 9–10
  Nixon and, 11, 13, 16, 17

opposition to, 10, 11–14,
  17, 25
peace negotiations, 17
support for, 14, 15–16, 17
television and, 12, 16–17
Viet Cong and, 10, 11
Vietnamization of, 17

The Waltons, 100
Warrior, Robert Allen, 44
Washington Post, 20, 100
Watergate, 19–21, 108
whales, 50
"Whole Lotta Love," 81
Wiley, Mason, 104
Wolfe, Tom, 15
Wolper, David, 99
women
  advertising and, 27–29
  employment of, 24, 30, 31,
  32
  fashion and, 64–68
  legal rights of, 29–30, 32–33
  liberation movement, 25–27,
  31, 33–35
  as portrayed in movies,
  101
  as portrayed on television,
  93–95
  sexual revolution and, 27
  sports and, 28
Women's Strike for Equality,
  25–26
Woodward, Bob, 20
Wounded Knee, 44, 45

youth
  activism of, 10, 13–15
  television and, 90, 94, 96, 98

Ziegler, Ron, 19–20

Picture Credits

Cover photos: (from left to right) Corbis-Bettmann, Corbis-Bettmann, Keith Myers/New York Times Co./Archive Photos

AP/Wide World Photos, 63

Archive Photos, 73

Archive Photos/The Platt Collection, 84

Library of Congress, 23, 107

Keith Meyers/New York Times Co./Archive Photos, 58

National Archives, 8, 9, 10, 18, 21

Paramount Pictures/Archive Photos, 103

Photofest, 6, 85, 87, 89, 91, 92, 94, 95, 97, 98, 99, 102

Joe Traver/New York Times Co./Archive Photos, 61

UPI Corbis-Bettmann, 14, 16, 24, 26, 28, 29, 31, 34, 36, 38, 40, 41, 42, 45, 46, 47, 49, 51, 55, 60, 65, 67, 69, 76, 79, 81, 104

Ricardo Watson/Archive Photos, 5

About the Author

Gail B. Stewart is the author of more than eighty books for children and young adults. She lives in Minneapolis, Minnesota, with her husband, Carl, and their sons, Ted, Elliot, and Flynn. When she is not writing, she spends her time reading, walking, and watching her sons play soccer.